APHROCHIC

Bryan Mason and Jeanine Hays

APHROCHIC

CELEBRATING THE LEGACY OF
THE BLACK FAMILY HOME

Photographs by Patrick Cline

Clarkson Potter/Publishers
New York

Published in the United States by Clarkson
Potter/Publishers, an imprint of Random House,
a division of Penguin Random House LLC, New York.
ClarksonPotter.com
RandomHouseBooks.com

CLARKSON POTTER is a trademark and POTTER with
colophon is a registered trademark of Penguin
Random House LLC.

Library of Congress Cataloging-in-Publication
Data is available upon request.

ISBN: 978-0-593-23400-6
Ebook ISBN: 978-0-593-23401-3

Printed in China

Principal Photographer: Patrick Cline
Additional Photographers: Chinasa Cooper and
Jochen Arndt
Editor: Angelin Borsics
Editorial Assistant: Darian Keels
Designer: Robert Diaz
Production Editor: Abby Oladipo
Production Manager: Phil Leung
Compositors: Merri Ann Morrell and
Zoe Tokushige
Copy Editors: Natalie Blachere and Diana Drew
Marketer: Andrea Portanova
Publicist: Natalie Yera

10 9 8 7 6 5 4 3 2 1

First Edition

FOR OUR ANCESTORS, WHO STARTED THIS JOURNEY, THOSE WHO ARE ON IT WITH US NOW, AND EVERYONE WHO WILL SEE IT THROUGH.

CONTENTS

A blend of African and Hawaiian pieces are on display, atop the piano in the home of Bridgid Coulter.

INTRODUCTION

> History, as nearly no one seems to know, is not merely something to be read. And it does not refer, merely, or even principally, to the past. On the contrary, the great force of history comes from the fact that we carry it within us, are unconsciously controlled by it in many ways, and history is literally present in all that we do.
>
> —James Baldwin, *Dark Days*

We all have a story of home, beginning with the first place that we remember. It travels with us, growing as we grow, written into our homes with colors, patterns, furniture, and accessories. In our first book, *REMIX*, we explored those elements and the ways that we use them in our homes to tell our story. In this book, we are excited to explore the story of home itself, those of the families featured here, and that of African Americans as a whole.

We at AphroChic are lovers of history. And while this is a design book, it's also a book about history, for as James Baldwin points out, the past is always with us, and we are formed by both the parts we include and by what gets left out. For too long, the Black family home has been left out of the story of America—a missing character. It's time to write the full story.

The Black family home is a vibe. More than just a place where people live, it's a feeling. It comes from the food that we eat, the music we hear, the stories we share. It comes from the elders in our families—the ones who teach us to act right, be quiet, and pay attention. The ones with the stories, recipes, and lessons that we never forget. Whether an apartment, a condo or a house, a new-build, or a generational home, the feeling is the same. Home is like "soul"—indescribable, but you know it when you feel it and you miss it when it's gone. Much of that feeling is carried in the unique aesthetic that defines African American design.

Like every part of a culture, design is shaped by history. The shape of American history has created a set of needs for African Americans, which are reflected in our homes. Much as we have with food, music, and dance, African Americans have used design as a way of meeting those needs. African American design is uniquely experiential in that it isn't defined by look as much as it is by feel. There are no defined color palettes or furniture styles. Instead, it uses a diverse array of approaches to craft environments that evoke feelings such as safety, control, visibility, celebration, and memory. Each of these plays an important role in the feeling of home that these spaces convey.

When asked what their homes mean to them, "safety" was the first response of every homeowner in this book. Life in America is not safe for Black people and never has been. While the sense of safety our homes provide is not the same as physical security, home is a respite from the psychological pressures of the outside world. For that reason, Black homes are filled with comfortable things and things that comfort.

> "Home is like 'soul'—indescribable, but you know it when you feel it and you miss it when it's gone."

Control, as an element of African American design, is about the ease with which our creative decisions are made. Home offers a space that doesn't have to be carved out, contended for, or defended once won. It doesn't ask us to explain ourselves, speak for our race, ignore its microaggressions, or be on call for teachable moments. No one ever asks to touch your home. In place of all that, home gives us the control we need to express and represent ourselves freely.

Visibility and representation are constant social battles for African Americans—as much a question of how and why we're seen as when and where we are seen. Home is a place apart from the scrutiny and stereotypes of the white gaze. And if we struggle to separate who we are from how we are seen, designing our homes can give us the space and means to address those issues in ways that not only showcase our stories and cultures but celebrate them as well.

Celebration may be the most important element of African American interior design. We do not define our culture by tragedy and oppression but by enduring hope, creativity, and joy. The embrace of color, art, and culture in our design creates a joyful place where the stories of a person, a family, and a people are celebrated and remembered.

Memory is the root of soul, and a vital part of African American design. Through design we both retain the past and contemporize it. Our designs recall the places we grew up in, our ancestral homes and

Opposite:
A collection of Balinese
fans in fuchsia and teal add
a colorful display to the
bedroom wall in the home of
Treci and Amir Smith.

the ancestors themselves, connecting our stories to the stories that came before. Memory is where African American design starts.

Because of how well it blends eras and aesthetics, African American design is strongly anti-thematic, valuing personal expression above all else. Like jazz improvisations or street style fashion, our design aesthetics are unique to each of us—a multitude of expressions connected through a variety of experiences that are shared but not identical. Within these experiences, home may be where we go to feel safe, welcome, and seen, but getting there has been difficult.

Beginning with Emancipation—and even before—the African American journey to home has been a hard-fought road, and never a straight route. We have built communities that were burned or destroyed by white supremacists; owned land that was stolen or from which we were driven away; established legal protections against discriminatory practices, only to see those protections rolled back until today, resulting in the lowest rate of homeownership among African Americans since the 1960s. Nevertheless, our journey is etched into the history of America. Its peaks and valleys have come at some of this nation's most crucial turning points. Because of that, it's a useful way to measure the nation's social, political, and economic steps, both forward and back. And yet, it's a story that hasn't really been told before now and it's important to consider why.

"At this point we leave Africa," Georg Hegel once wrote, "not to mention it again. For it is no historical part of the World; it has no movement or development to exhibit." Remembered widely as one of the architects of modern Western philosophy—and less widely as a framer of modern racism—Hegel's statement continues to shape popular notions about the place of Black people in history. The sentiment hasn't lasted because it's true; it lasts because it justifies actions and normalizes power relationships built on the lie of a biological racial hierarchy. It took time. Racism as we know it today is not ancient, but it didn't form overnight. Maintaining it requires the work of generations. Creating it required the hard work of forgetting.

Forgetting is a complicated and difficult act. The erasure of an entire people from history demands more than ignoring the highlights of their past. The present must also be obscured through stereotypes, misrepresentations, and omissions. In its representations as part of Black life in America, the Black family home has been subjected to all three.

Our homes rarely appear in popular media. There are few design books dedicated to our aesthetics, and few studies explore the role of our homes in our communities or the world at large. As such, Black homes are generally thought to fall into three common tropes: that all

Black people live in impoverished homes; that the only Black people who don't live in some form of poverty are celebrities, musicians, actors, or athletes; and that Black people who are not celebrities but don't live in the ghetto occupy houses that are "normal," and therefore essentially identical to the homes of white people. Like all stereotypes, these reduce the true diversity of Black life to a few acceptable possibilities. And while the impact of such misrepresentations on the lives and opportunities of individual Black people is well-established, they are equally significant to American society as a whole in ways that begin to explain why the history of Black American homes is missing from the larger American narrative in the first place.

> "The omission of the Black family home is one of many linchpins holding together a collection of American myths."

The omission of the Black family home is one of many linchpins holding together a collection of American myths, such as "bootstrapping"—the idea that everyone in America pulls themselves up by their own bootstraps with no external help and success is determined by self-reliance. Closely aligned with this is the myth of personal responsibility, which argues that individual achievements are entirely the result of personal choices, without regard to external social circumstances, such as the institution of racism. While these ideas are vital to the American identity, the history of our nation tells a different story.

Over the years, the United States has often offered assistance, building programs, and other help to Americans seeking to own homes. Almost all of these programs have, to some extent, excluded African Americans who have also faced discriminatory practices in banking and real estate as well as disparities in wages and inheritances. The outcome of this history is reflected in the wealth gap that exists between Black and white communities, predicated largely on the gap in homeownership that has existed for more than a century and continues to grow today. So perhaps the most significant consequence of the Black family home's absence from history is that we are encouraged to view the current deficit in African American homeownership as the single result of the choices of individual Black people, rather than as one outcome of generations of disenfranchisement.

As you read this book, you will see the stunning diversity of the Black American experience. In sixteen beautiful home portraits we've collected the stories of artists and actors, small business owners, and expats living abroad in homes ranging from svelte Harlem apartments to sprawling North Carolina ranches. As we celebrate the beauty of these experiences, we also offer a brief history of the African American journey to home beginning with the first days of Emancipation and Reconstruction and continuing to the present crises of the Great Recession and COVID-19.

The homeowners' stories show us our connection with this history and the importance of what generations before us worked to establish. Many had grandparents who traveled the country during the Great Migration. Some were even able to trace their families back to the plantation on which they were enslaved; some benefit today from the work of an ancestor freed centuries ago. Others had parents who immigrated from other nations or are immigrants themselves. At some point in their stories, many experienced discrimination, either in determining where their families could live, lingering in the deeds to properties they bought, or hindering their own attempts to buy a home.

There is a reason we've chosen to include so much history in a book about design. While the home portraits show us the triumph of individuals, the larger history reveals the travails of a people. Where one shows us unique variety, the other gives us shared context. Look closely enough at the struggle and you'll see the joy. Look deeply enough into the joy and you'll see the work that goes into finding and maintaining it. Taken together, they reveal some important truths.

The struggle and survival that characterize the story of the Black family home are not two sides of the same coin; rather, they are the same story viewed from different angles: one as close as a single household, the other at a distance of generations. Moreover, that there are currently so few African American homeowners is not incidental, nor is it solely the result of individual choices made by Black people. It is only the most recent outcome of the larger history of an ongoing system of intentional disenfranchisement aimed at the Black community in America. As such it is only within that wider context that the present moment can be truly understood.

The Black experience is broad. Within these chapters we invite you to explore stories happening in America and beyond, highlighting homes purchased with wealth built over generations, new homes full of inherited heirlooms, homes off the beaten path, and homes that showcase the diversity of our work, creativity, and style as Black people.

The Journey Home: EMANCIPATION AND RECONSTRUCTION

The African American experience of home does not begin with Emancipation. Even through the long years of American slavery, there were a wide variety of Black lives. In Philadelphia, free African Americans numbered more than 1,000 by the end of the Revolutionary War. Black people, held nominally as slaves by various Native American tribes, participated heavily in their societies, freely intermarrying and in some cases rising to lead their communities. Free African Americans owned enslaved people— as well as white indentured servants—in every state that countenanced the practice. Others became merchants and ministers, cowboys and even pirates. All had their adventures and struggles while negotiating the constant threat of capture and enslavement.

For the vast majority of African Americans, however, the long journey toward home begins with the end of the Civil War. Prior to that, the struggles of finding a home were already apparent to those freed by the chaos and turmoil of the conflict. Initially regarded as "contraband," and returned to their enslavers by the Union Army, hundreds of thousands would later huddle in refugee camps erected in and around army bases throughout the South. Some worked without pay or were hired out by the Army. Most existed in various states of homelessness. In Washington, DC, many who escaped the South were interned at the Old Capitol Prison, making an immediate transition from slavery to incarceration. By the end of the war, an additional 4 million people would be in need of new homes as the reunified nation turned to the task of Reconstruction.

In 1865, just two months before the end of the war, the Bureau of Refugees, Freedmen and Abandoned Lands, or the "Freedman's Bureau," was created. Its purpose, among other things, was to provide homes and employment to those newly freed. For a brief while, the US government became an ally to the Southern African American community, negotiating labor contracts, creating schools, establishing courts, and attempting to stand between the community and the violence of white militias, insurgents, and mobs. It also tried to address the growing need for housing. Abraham Lincoln ordered that small plots of land be made available to former slaves for purchase at tax sales. However, as most lacked any form of income, the effort had little effect.

The people held in the Old Capitol Prison were eventually moved to an adjacent series of tenement buildings. Later, housing would be offered for freed African Americans in a series of converted Army barracks throughout the area. Through it all, conditions remained dismal. Food was scarce and disease rampant, in some places killing as many as one in seven. Employment, often on government farms, was a requisite of housing and, though salaries were paid, the majority of each household's income was repaid to the Army in rent and expenses each month. The Army, meanwhile, made a substantial sum by selling the crops produced by Black labor.

Treatment of the freedmen by whites alternated between the overbearing paternalism of the housing administrators and the rising violence of nearby neighbors. The former ranged from random inspections and occupancy restrictions to compulsory marriages for any couples wanting to reside together. The latter included random attacks on Black residents by white assailants leading to an open siege of an entire building. While the smaller attacks drew no attention from the police, the siege was carried out with open support from local officers. Residents of the tenements were vocal and active in their opposition to both, writing letters and holding political meetings on the grounds to establish their rights as free people.

Ultimately, the efforts of the Freedman's Bureau failed through a combination of ambivalence from within and opposition from without. The legislation that created the bureau originally permitted its commissioner, General Oliver Howard (for whom Howard University is named), to provide as many as 40 acres of land to each freedman from the territory taken from Southern plantation owners during the war. A seeming reiteration of General Sherman's famous "40 acres and mule" order (which was recommended by twenty Black community leaders in Georgia, though their recommendation didn't mention a mule), it would have provided 400,000 acres of land to African American families.

However, following Lincoln's assassination in April 1865, Andrew Johnson became president. A staunch opponent of Black homeownership, Johnson issued a proclamation facilitating the return of confiscated lands back into white Southern hands. Johnson remained an implacable adversary of the bureau, which was formally disbanded in 1872. His policies effectively replaced the possibility of landownership and self-reliance with sharecropping and peonage, the foundations of which had already been laid by the exploitative practices of the Army.

As Southern economic and political power reverted to the former Confederates, new Black Codes were enacted, setting the stage for the Jim Crow era to come. Vagrancy laws outlawed unemployment, allowing any freedman who refused a sharecropping contract to be arrested and hired out. Proof of employment replaced freedom papers as necessary documentation and filled prisons with those who didn't have them. Concurrently, the innovation of convict leasing cemented the prison system as the unspoken replacement for slavery, renting prisoners out as laborers.

The lost promise of the Freedman's Bureau together with Johnson's empowerment of former plantation owners largely reestablished the previous power structure, trapping many—but by no means all—African Americans in generations of poverty and pushing the dream of homeownership that much further away.

HEIRLOOM HOMES

From single pieces to whole rooms filled with memories, these are homes with history. Some of the heirlooms that fill these spaces have been handed down, while others are pieces specially created to commemorate a crucial moment in the past. These are homes that tell the story of generations.

Ariene and Daren Bethea's art collection includes expressionist pieces along with a mix of hand-moulded and carved sculptures that were inherited from Ariene's mother.

DRAWING FASHION *The Art of Kenneth Paul Block*

PAUL SUEPAT AND TOMMY WONG: ARTIST IN WONDERLAND

FOR NEW YORK ARTIST PAUL SUEPAT, going home means walking into a world of his own making, one that he has worked for a very long time to build. His home is an homage to different aspects of his life. Handmade sculptural flowers are a reminder of his grandmother. The library, a loving re-creation of a room in his godparents' Manhattan home. And whimsical elements throughout are a nod to his own journey to freedom.

Paul's story—and the story of his home—begins in Jamaica. For the first twelve years of his life, and intermittently thereafter, he lived with his paternal grandmother. "Owning her own home was very special to her," he reflects. "She had kind of eccentric tastes—like a vanity with all kinds of plastic flowers and figurines. It was funny, but she really made me appreciate the things we have at home." While his parents lived and ran a business in another neighborhood, one that was taking a turn for the worse, they sent him to his grandmother to keep him safe. He credits her for giving him the basic disciplines in life. "My grandmother taught me how to eat, how to sit at the table, how to appreciate small things. She really made me pay attention to things. And I have this discipline of creating things because that's what I got from her." Paul's grandmother was also one of his first artistic influences.

"She was just always making things," he remembers. "She used to

Right:
The office is home to a
collection of art and objects.
Paul's pieces hang on the walls
and sit among work by Basquiat
and a Warhol-esque chicken
gumbo soup can sculpture.

Above:
A stunning collection of modern classic furnishings are assembled in the library, including Ligne Roset's Confluences sofa, an original Gae Aulenti "Pipistrello" lamp, and a Herman Miller office chair.

Opposite:
The bookshelves from Paul's aunt and uncle's home were lovingly taken apart, transported, and installed in Paul and Tommy's home office.

make flowers from raffia, like these little pom-poms on a stick. I used to sit and watch her make flowers all night. And in the morning she would go downtown to sell them in the market. I think that's where I got that whole idea of making stuff with my hands."

His other great childhood inspiration was nature. His grandmother's house, near the mountains, backed up to the woods. As a boy, Paul would lie on the ground for hours, shoes off, and feel the world around him. "I found it very free being in nature," he muses. "I liked the textures a lot. I loved playing in the dirt. I think that's part of my attraction to sculpture and painting: I like to feel textures." It was a place for him to dream. "We had tons of trees. Mango and plum and cherry and avocado trees. I would lay out under them, and I would dream about deities and gods. I'd make up stories about these special people who lived in the woods and imagine that I was going to find them. It was my little bit of an escape, and it's one of the things I miss most about growing up."

Following his grandmother's example, Paul expressed his creativity in various ways. "I didn't think I was an artist," he says. "It took me a while to realize that." But he dabbled constantly in creative pursuits.

Right:
The living room has an *Alice in Wonderland* feel to it with oversized sculptural elements, futuristic furnishings, and Paul's vivid and textural art.

A gecko sculpture coming down the wall
is an ode to Paul's Caribbean roots.

Columns that frame the entry to the living room were painted a bright shade of blue by Paul. Original to the prewar home, they feel fresh and modern in the electric shade.

"When I was a child, I put my bed on the floor and I used two rocks from the garden as a bedside table. I guess I was a minimalist," he says with a laugh. As he grew, his creativity evolved. High-concept bedroom arrangements gave way to creating his own clothes. By the time he was ready for college, art seemed like a more viable path. He was encouraged to attend the Edna Manley College of the Visual and Performing Arts. "It really kind of opened my eyes and showed me that there's a possibility here that I could be an artist."

His first canvases were T-shirts. While selling his fashions, Paul began looking for galleries to show the art he was creating. Fashion grew faster at first, and his enterprise soon developed into a shop with a studio in the back. Recognition for his art wasn't far behind, however. While still at school, Paul signed with the prestigious Mutual Gallery in Kingston. "I had quite a few very good shows there." Early success brought a number of important lessons for the young artist. "One time, the gallerist was telling me that I had someone interested in buying one of my paintings, but they wanted me to take the frame off," he remembers. "I had put a lot of work into the frames so I didn't want to." Paul remained unmoved even after being told that the buyer was married to someone famous. When he found out that the someone was Harry Belafonte, his tone quickly changed. "I said, 'Oh, okay. I think it's fine,'" he says, laughing. "That's when I realized this was serious, and I had to let my ego go."

"My grandmother taught me how to eat, how to sit at the table, how to appreciate small things."

While becoming known as an artist was great, his growing popularity brought unwanted attention as well. "With publicity came the idea that I was gay," he explains. "And I was harassed a lot." The situation built and escalated over time to the point that it threatened his life. "One night some guys came to my home," he remembers emotionally, "and I had to leave. That's how I came to America. I left with just two bags and came because I had to." Narrowly escaping, Paul left his life in Jamaica, the artwork, the studio, everything, and sought asylum in the United States. He arrived first in Florida, living with his sister and working odd jobs, most of which he hated. But they helped him build toward his ultimate goal. "I knew New York was my destiny," he states. "I'd been to New York a few times," he explains, "and I loved it. All my friends had two jobs and small apartments, but I wanted to be there." Eventually, he made the drive from South Beach to Manhattan.

Landing in the West Village, Paul was able to live with his godparents. "My godparents are Bill Schaap and Ellen Ray," he says.

In the dining room, a vintage Le
Corbusier dining table and chairs by
Mario Botta sit atop a rug hand-painted
by Paul. The sculptural chandelier
above the table was also concepted
by Paul.

Opposite:
The bedroom is filled with
whimsical moments. A chair
featuring an extra-long back
and a paint-can sculpture add
moments of eccentricity to
the space.

"They were lawyers, then journalists, and then publishers. They published the book that inspired the movie *JFK*." While working in Jamaica years earlier, the pair had become friends of Paul's family. The connection remained strong over the years, and when he arrived in the city they were waiting. "They were very kind and open. They said, 'Just come and spend some time with us and see what you want to do.'"

Upon reaching New York, he was able to begin again as an artist. "It was difficult here at first because when you're Jamaican, they think all you should be painting is palm trees," he remarks. "I think a lot of people don't realize that just being a Black or Brown artist doesn't mean you have to paint a specific way." Paul's art, which is often surreal and plays with the line between painting and sculpture, fell far outside of expectations. Fortunately, his godparents were people of varied interests and meaningful connections. "They were really political," he remembers. "They'd given money to the Black Panthers and defended protesters in court. When I lived with them, they were writing a magazine." In addition to their political interests, they were avid art lovers. "They had a gallery of their own. And they'd always said that if I ever came to New York they would show my stuff. I had a show at their space, and then it kind of developed from there."

Since then, Paul's work has been shown in dozens of exhibitions and public art installations in venues like the Brooklyn Museum and Vanderbilt Hall in New York's Grand Central Terminal. "I always keep a piece from each show," he says, "just to remember." Even more important than a place to show his art, however, Paul's godparents gave him a sense of home. "They saved me," he states simply. "They took me in and loved me and really nurtured me and it was my first experience of being in New York."

But the artist was still in search of a place of his own. "My father's brother had a furniture shop in Flatbush in the 1970s. So when I came to New York, I would come to Flatbush and I would go to parties in Bed-Stuy. The first time I remember coming to Bed-Stuy it was like something was drawing me to it," he says. "I was just like, 'This feels like Kingston.' So, eventually, I came back, and I loved it. I opened a little café for a while. And then I met my partner." His partner, Dr. Tommy Wong, is a celebrated emergency medical doctor and educator. "I like to say *partner*," he affirms, "even though we're married, because that's how I look at a relationship. We're partners, we help each other, whether emotionally or whatever else it may be." For more than a decade, they've been each other's home, eventually finding a space where Paul could build the world he'd been seeing since he was a child lying in the woods behind his grandmother's house.

When Paul and Tommy found their dream home in Bed-Stuy, it had

Opposite:
The garden includes a series
of handmade sculptures
by Paul. They feel like an
extension of the garden he
grew up playing in as a child,
where his grandmother would
handcraft items.

seen better days. Abandoned for years, a fire had gutted much of the top floor. But none of that mattered. All Paul could see was its potential. "The house was a mess," he admits, "but I love to work, to do things. And so I just got involved in it. I did a lot of stuff myself, and I was involved in every detail." Rebuilding his home from scratch pulled together all of the scattered pieces of Paul's journey. To start, working with what so many other people would think of as nothing put him right into his comfort zone. "I think you're more creative when you have nothing," he states. It also gave him space to pay homage to the people who had saved him. The upstairs library is a close re-creation of the same room in his godparents' home, composed almost entirely of objects he inherited from them after their passing—including the bookcases, books, art, furniture, and fireplace.

The sculpture garden out back is a remembrance of his grandmother's home, lacking all of the texture of raw nature, but filled with tangible realizations of his dreams. Oversized flowers accent the organic greenery while sculptures of the "special people" Paul imagined living in the woods peek out from different angles. Inside, the rooms are likewise filled with imaginings, both his own work and the works of other artists that he cherishes. "I always wanted to have interesting things around me," he intones. "That's how the whole idea of art started for me. I couldn't afford them, so I would make them. My art started as things I wanted to have for myself. And then other people started to like them, too."

Brought together, these elements are the foundation of the whimsical world Paul has created. It's a constantly evolving representation of the mind behind it. "I'm always struggling between the openness of nature and the urban-ness of New York," he says, "because there's always that fight to get out of whatever box you're in. So I want people to look at things in a different way—and I'm always trying to see if I can push it a little bit further."

Throughout his journey Paul has always kept home as the most important thing. Using art and memories to create his own private wonderland is ultimately about finally capturing a feeling of freedom and security that he's been chasing since he was a child. "As a child, I was left by my parents, and I've always felt kind of abandoned," he says. "I know that home is important because I've been made to feel not-at-home. I've had to leave home, to search for home, to be without home—and that was hard. So for me home is everything. It's what you do everything for, where you can be what you want and do what you want. Home is an escape. It's the thing I need to see so that I can face the rest of the world."

SHAWNA FREEMAN: HONORING THE PAST

CHARLOTTE, NORTH CAROLINA

SHAWNA FREEMAN HAS A COTTON TREE. It stands against the far wall of her front parlor. She made it herself, weaving together cotton flowers and fig branches to create a stunning display that tells the story of her family's special relationship to the plant. It's a story she loves to tell. "My grandparents on my mother's side were sharecroppers in Louisiana. Working the land in exchange for food and lodging was the only way to live," she recounts.

Like many of those enslaved in the Deep South, Shawna's family went from picking cotton for plantation owners to sharecropping the crop for landowners, eventually becoming landowners themselves. A loan program offered by the Truman administration in the 1940s offered Black people funds for purchasing land. The loan had to be repaid quickly, but it allowed Shawna's grandparents to obtain a small parcel. Because it was what they knew best, they used that land to grow cotton and to raise their fourteen children. Over time the family business grew from its first parcel to encompass 120 acres. Through them, Shawna's grandparents laid the groundwork for their children's futures, ensuring that each of them received a college education. "So I grew up hearing stories of picking cotton but because it was how my family achieved financial independence," she says.

The entertainment room has a playful array of colors and textures. Shawna painted the ceiling gold to ground the brightly hued space.

In every room in her home Shawna
is honoring her roots. The guest
bedroom is designed to be a nod
to her Louisiana heritage.

Atop the bamboo bookshelf is a photo
of Shawna and Muhammad Ali. Her father
captured the meeting between the young
girl and the global icon.

Shawna's embrace of color can be seen throughout her home. The living room is a play on neutrals, but a bright yellow sofa injects a dose of color into the space.

A green thumb is on display in the home's dining area. Plants brighten the eat-in area and the natural wood furnishings are a complement.

The fifth of nine children, her father also came from a large family that believed in progress through education. "None of my grandparents have high school diplomas," she explains, "but all of their kids went to college." While Shawna's mother would go on to pursue a career as an educator, she credits her father, who became an architect for the Navy, with shaping much of her own sense of design.

For the first ten years of Shawna's life, the family shared a 1970s-style home in Virginia Beach. Her parents would divorce when she was eleven, but she vividly recalls the home they had together. She remembers shag carpets, rooms of many colors, and sliding down stairs in laundry baskets. Most of all she remembers the things her father added.

"Dad was the one who made the decisions about decorating the house," Shawna remembers. "We didn't have much money, but when you have creativity you can do a lot of things." Her father painted several murals throughout the house, including a silhouette-based faux wallpaper and a Mickey Mouse mural in her room. He also built her a treehouse in the backyard, which became a neighborhood hangout. Her father's creativity created an environment in which Shawna felt free to explore on her own. "I wasn't allowed to jump around on the furniture or anything," she clarifies, "but home just felt like my domain, my place to be creative and play."

A teacher, her mother added to the family aesthetic through global exploration. Her mother received several Fulbright grants, and she never failed to bring home mementos from her trips to Egypt and Japan. Likewise, her father's work as a naval architect took him around the world, designing bases in Kenya, among other places. "The trips were commemorative of their professional successes. The things they brought back became extra meaningful and formed the foundation of our home."

Family heirlooms were equally plentiful. "My parents are very close to their siblings," she confides. "A lot of what they treasured were things that belonged to family members. My dad had his brother's hammer framed in a box in his office."

Shawna's craftsman home, in Charlotte, North Carolina, is a masterwork of self-expression through design, pulling from all of the various stages of her life to present a clear image of the woman she is now. After fourteen years in New York City, she made the decision to purchase a home of her own. "I was thirty by the time I had my own apartment," she explains. Returning home after obtaining a psychology degree from Princeton, she lived with an aunt in New York while

"None of my grandparents have high school diplomas, but all of their kids went to college."

pursuing a master's degree. But everything changed when she left New York for North Carolina and a house of her own.

A wondrous journey through color from room to room, the home's first steps are deceptively serene: a white hallway that feels like the first steps into a chic New York art gallery, hung with paintings that offer a striking color palette of pinks and blues. "That is something I brought from my childhood home," Shawna says of the love of art that defines her home. "My parents embraced original art as well as pieces from friends, and I've done the same here."

At the end of the hallway a small sitting room has been transformed into a beautiful parlor with black walls, brilliant art, and a vintage emerald velvet sofa that ranks among her favorite pieces in the home. "Pretty much all of the pieces I love are vintage," she offers. The room is also home to her handmade cotton tree.

Past the parlor, the floor plan opens up to the living area. Built-in bookshelves are guarded by Alastair, a much-loved and life-sized sandstone greyhound statue. The shelves are less a place for storing books and more a display for heirlooms and favorite things—the objects placed there connect to several significant places and events in Shawna's life, including a glass case containing the shoes that she wore on 9/11, still caked in the dust and debris that covered the city that day as she fled.

Up the stairs is where she lets her hair down, Shawna's personality shining through in each room. "The upstairs really is just for me and my close friends," she explains. That sense of separation allowed her to begin experimenting with bold ideas in her design at a point when she wasn't sure if they were things anyone else should see.

Starting with a small upstairs room that hadn't seen any use, she envisioned an office that would indulge her creative side away from her corporate job. It was the perfect place to experiment with color. "My feeling was that if it didn't work, I could just close the door," she says, laughing. But her bright fuchsia gamble paid off with a strikingly energetic space that she accented with earth tones and leopard prints. New York makes its presence felt with text art featuring the iconic "Can I kick it?" call and response from the legendary rap group A Tribe Called Quest. It's a perfect companion to a mood board that includes everything from postcards and Mardi Gras masks to images of Nelson Mandela, MLK, and W.E.B. DuBois. Shawna quickly realized that she had created a monster. "Walking in there was just incredible," she recalls. "It was addictive. I needed to do it again." Fortunately, her home had rooms to spare.

Across from her girl cave, another room needed a new life. Starting the space with a deep blue accent wall, the color quickly grew to

Opposite:
The main bedroom is a cozy
and enveloping space. Shawna
painted the walls a deep green
and brought in more warmth
with vintage tortoiseshell
side tables by Henredon.

envelop the entire room. When that wasn't enough, Shawna took it a step further, painting the ceiling in gold to complete the jewel box look. The two colors continue to play throughout the room, woven in through art and accessories, including framed fabrics and a gold coffee table. This is one of Shawna's more worldly spaces, with gold images of the Buddha mixing with masks from West Africa, poufs from North Africa, and handwoven fans and bowls.

"It's harder for me to feel the soul in a room without color," she explains. But the colorful environments of the upstairs are more than the expression of a personal aesthetic. For Shawna, color is an heirloom, a remembrance of her childhood home and the world her father created for her. "Dad really was the primary decorator," she reminisces. "Every room had a different color."

Other remembrances are scattered throughout the home. Like color, plants are a strong reminder of Shawna's father, who passed away in 2020. While her own collection of plants, concentrated in the dining room and upstairs bathroom, is considerable, Shawna is quick to allow that it pales in comparison to the collection he had. "He had zillions," she says. "He had several that were over thirty years old."

In her bedroom, framed Egyptian papyri hang, a reminder of her mother's summer there when Shawna was ten. "She brought back all kinds of things. We had a lot of papyrus on the walls." A step back from her bolder efforts, the room nevertheless energizes through its use of pattern and pops of deep emerald green. A bright fuchsia arrangement of flowers on the table might be a portent of things to come, but Shawna is wary of giving every room a different look. "It's been an evolution," she allows, "but I don't want it to look like a quilt."

There is a well-known saying in the Black community that we are our ancestors' wildest dreams. When Shawna's grandparents bought their first plot of land and sowed those first seeds, they dreamed of a better life for their family. And that dream has been fulfilled. All of the heirlooms in Shawna's home are part of her family's legacy. And all of them serve to reinforce the lesson she takes from the oldest one. "There's a hat in the guest room made out of corn husks that was my grandmother's. They didn't have any hats when they were out in the fields. To me it symbolizes resourcefulness. They were able to make something out of nothing. And I'm here now because they did."

ALEXANDER SMALLS: GROWING IN THE GARDEN

THERE IS AN OLD SAYING—that great things come from humble beginnings. Alexander Smalls has done great things. One of an exclusive community of African American opera singers to make a name for himself internationally, he won awards for his singing before leaving the stage for the kitchen, opening several restaurants to great acclaim and more awards. Along the way, his cookbooks have redefined the genre, mixing lessons on Black history with recipes and personal reflections to show the crucial role that food plays in culture. Though Harlem has been his home for decades, Alexander's beginnings lie in rural South Carolina, both the Upcountry where he grew up, and the Lowcountry from which his father's family culture hailed. Though far from the stages he would later command, his early days were hardly humble. In fact, the great things Alexander would achieve were never about growing past his beginnings but about making the rest of the world as large and full of possibilities as the home that he grew up in.

"I was born at home," he says, recounting a time and a place he can't remember. "My mother was dressing to go to the doctor and I was in a hurry. She got as far as the living room. My father delivered me." The first home to live in his memory would come years later, when he was in kindergarten. In a small complex, a two-bedroom apartment held Alexander, his parents, and two other siblings. "We were all over the

Above:
The home's Harlem Renaissance-era vibe is a tribute to Alexander's aunt and uncle. Vibrant colors, evocative art, and moody lighting create the feeling of a 1920s salon.

Opposite:
The home is filled with vintage heirlooms. In the living room, his mother's fur coat is draped over the black-and-white Chippendale sofa.

place," he remembers, but it was only for a short while. Before long, the family took on a much larger enterprise.

Purchasing a lot, Alexander's parents began building a home of their own. And while the project was too big to hide from the children, they couldn't be completely open about it, either. "We thought my father was the foreman overseeing a house being built for a friend," he remembers. "My mother knew that if she told us, especially me, the town would know. Because if you wanted to get something out, tell Alexander." The children had no idea until they were ready to move in. "One day they brought us over and said, 'This is your new home.'"

For Alexander's parents, building a home from the ground up was a financial investment. It was a place to raise their children and give them a foundation for everything that they might achieve in life. But there was more. Homeownership granted far greater ability to dictate the look of the place, and their home became a massive canvas for expressing a family creative aesthetic that was already highly developed in other ways.

"We were the best dressed people on the block," he says with a laugh. "My father was kind of a dandy. The kind of guy who would go

and buy four suits at a time—with six pairs of shoes. My father was an upholsterer, shoemaker, and—he wasn't a tailor but, because he was an upholsterer, he could make patterns and he could fit." Similarly, Alexander's mother was a dressmaker who made most of the clothes that she and her children wore. "Not having a whole lot of money," Alexander says, "one of the gifts they gave themselves was constantly redressing our home."

Changes to the look of the Smalls family home were seasonal, and they were extensive. Alexander's father frequently made new slipcovers for all of the furniture, which was constantly being repositioned. His mother's skill with fabrics translated into a love of curtains that he inherited. Like their clothes, interior design for the Smalls family was an exercise in self-expression and self-worth. The highest standard of quality was the lowest expectation. "It was always pristine," he remembers, "always magazine-ready. They took a great deal of pride. And the living room was off-limits."

Despite being kept out of the living room, Alexander remembers the home as a place of warmth and limitless possibility. "My parents were so embracing and generous and providing," he says gently, as if the memory itself were precious and fragile. "Our home was always gracious and well appointed. It was a loving home."

The relationship between Alexander's path in life and where he started is extraordinary. Most people are formed to some extent by the spaces in which they grow up. For Alexander, his remarkable life and the spaces that he would create for himself were almost entirely shaped by the geometry of his youth.

The world that made Alexander Smalls was essentially a pyramid, albeit with a four-point layout. At the pinnacle sat his paternal grandfather's home. At the base lay the house his parents built, across half an acre of cultivated garden. Completing the pyramid at the other side of the garden was a third house, belonging to his uncle and aunt. The fourth space was the garden itself. All four would have a hand in who he would eventually become.

"That's how I would basically experience my day-to-day," he reflects. "My grandfather's house at one point, my uncle's at another, my parents' at the other end, and the garden in between." The garden was one of the most important spaces of Alexander's youth. Not only did it symbolize his life as a midpoint between three major nodes of influence, but, much more important, it was also where he spent time with his grandfather.

"I worshipped my grandfather," he confesses. "He was kind of noble and statuesque and bigger than life. Though he was only about five feet eight inches, he just seemed huge. Even as I grew older and taller, he never lost his stature." While his mother was also a gardener who

Alexander's dining room is central
to the interior. A lover of hosting
gatherings, Alexander designed the
space to host intimate dinners with
family and friends.

maintained a beautiful bed of flowers in front of their house, Alexander was always drawn to the back, where the vegetables were.

"The thing about being in the vegetable garden," Alexander reflects, "was the harvest. I was with my grandfather, who would work the land and tell the family stories and lore. He'd talk about his parents and it would take on a whole kind of intimate moment that we shared." The son of enslaved parents, Alexander's grandfather came from a time just after Emancipation, but a long way from civil rights. "He grew up in the shadow of much of that and much of that made him the proud man he was," Alexander notes. Along with the family lore, Alexander absorbed lessons on history and culture, including the impact that West African culture and the trans-Atlantic slave trade had on the Lowcountry cuisine that was the family mainstay.

> "I understood the power and the beauty and the artistry of the world, and I started to bring all of that home."

A very early interest in Alexander's development was also taken by his uncle, a chef, and his aunt, a classical pianist. Both had been noted creatives in New York during the Harlem Renaissance. Following that period, and without children of their own, they decided to return to the South to be closer to family and to take part in the upbringing of the family's next generation. Avid fans of the opera, they would be Alexander's first introduction to a new world in which he would eventually carve his own space.

The memory brings an instant smile. "My uncle bought me a piano," he says with a grin, "because they had designed my life." Just as his grandfather did with his stories, Alexander's aunt and uncle poured all of their creativity and culture into their young nephew. "Much to my father's displeasure," he remembers, "because now he was competing with his favorite brother and sister-in-law for my attention. And because they didn't have kids, they just took me over."

But competing for attention never took precedence over encouraging Alexander to be whatever he could dream of, and quickly his dreams turned entirely to music. After a brief life in the living room, the piano found its way into Alexander's bedroom, where it replaced his bed.

"I decided that I needed my own studio," he says, laughing. "I told my parents to move the piano into my bedroom, and replace my bed with a pullout sofa so that I could be the artist that I just knew that I was." The encouragement paid off, and, looking back, Alexander sees that the reason he always believed he could do anything was because no one had ever once told him that what he wanted couldn't be done.

"The greatest gift my parents ever gave me was that they never said no to the things that they understood were important to me. When I walked in the house and said I was going to be a Black opera singer, mother clutched her pearls and my father fell to the floor. They were looking for me to go be a doctor, a lawyer, even the president, but a singer? And opera? They didn't know anyone who did that." But even with no frame of reference and full knowledge of what the world could muster against him, their faith in their son prevailed. "They empowered me, no matter what, even though I know they were thinking that my aunt and uncle had ruined my life," he says, laughing.

Time would prove his parents' faith more accurate than their fears. Alexander graduated from the University of North Carolina School of the Arts and the prestigious Curtis Institute of Music in Philadelphia before beginning his career in singing. Along the way, he would earn numerous awards while living, performing, and studying in Italy, Germany, and Paris. When he walked away abruptly—"I hit the glass ceiling," he explains simply—he combined culinary studies at La Varenne with a lifetime of experience in cooking Lowcountry cuisine to create a chain of successful restaurants and pen a series of genre-expanding cookbooks.

Since returning to America, New York has been home to Alexander as well as his restaurants. Harlem, in particular, has been both a refuge and a source of continual inspiration. Yet, despite being so far from South Carolina, his apartment remains the sum of his influences, punctuated by memories of his experiences. From one perspective, the home is Alexander in miniature. From another, it's him writ large. It's a sophisticated 1920s-style Harlem salon with a South Carolina Lowcountry kitchen. Its soul is his soul. Its contents a summary of him.

From room to room the color of the walls is one of Alexander's strongest homages to home. A sunny yellow carries from the entry hallway to the kitchen, giving way to a deep red in the music room. "My earliest aesthetic still lives," he admits. "My mother loved yellow earth tones, burgundy, golds." Similarly, his parents' influence is felt in the various fabrics that adorn his home. Drapery is everywhere, offering shade from windows and acting as dividers between rooms. "An ode to my mother," the chef confesses. "She was hugely into drapes and would bring in the softer side—the silks and linens. My father would bring in the wools, velvet, fabrics with texture, and they married their aesthetics."

The voices of Alexander's aunt and uncle resonate throughout the space as well. It's not by coincidence that for decades, the restaurateur has made Harlem his home. Like so many other things, the couple planted those seeds in their nephew many years ago, along with a love for opera, Shakespeare, Langston Hughes, and art. "They used to have this fabulous, chic apartment in Harlem," he reminisces. They were

Opposite:
Alexander's home office
is a symphony of bright hues,
with vivid art on the wall
and jewel-toned furnishings.

sophisticated. They knew art. They knew artists. They did the same as my parents, except with art and antiques." Their touch is felt in the abundance of paintings, posters, and photos that cover nearly every inch of wall space in each room and in the army of books that spill from bookshelves and stack beneath coffee tables.

But the home of a world-traveling, universally celebrated singer, chef, and author is more than the sum of where he came from; it's also a chronicle of where he went. "Opera was the vehicle," he explains. "It thrust me from the Black side of town to the white side of town, and then from the white side of town to out of town. And as I began to live in this expanded narrative, being touted as this artist—even more so in Europe because I was Black—coming to see the power of my complexion instead of the negative and the prejudice, I understood the power and the beauty and the artistry of the world, and I started to bring all of that home."

The things that Alexander collected from his travels are things that his family would appreciate. Books, fabrics, art—his own unique, globalized take on a family aesthetic that he inherited, even as it was being created. In his home, reminders of family mix seamlessly with pieces from around the world. "I have one of my mother's fur coats draped over a Chippendale," the singer muses, "and her stole draped over another." His collection also includes his mother's china and wedding silver, and a number of his father's hats. The fabrics he brings home from travel are used to create new garments or to update old furniture. "That's the way I keep my parents alive," he confesses. "There's not one thing in this apartment that has cloth on it that wasn't designed or created specifically for me."

The home also contains mementos collected from the restaurateur's early career, including ceiling fans and barstools from his first restaurant. The bar itself is from his second. "Some people call it a little museum," he reflects contentedly. "Some people think it's a men's club. But it's cozy."

Alexander Smalls was born into a home where he learned that everything is possible. Since leaving, he has lived many lives, each one dedicated to demonstrating that truth to the rest of the world. Through his talents on the stage and in the kitchen, he has created space for himself in worlds not accustomed to Black presence, while making it clear that we had been there all along. But for Alexander, it's not about where you go, but how you get there. "I tell people all the time, 'Don't get caught up in the destination; the point is the journey.' It is everything that gets you there. If all goes well, the destination is the icing on the cake."

ARIENE AND DAREN BETHEA: MATERIAL MEMORIES

CHARLOTTE, NORTH CAROLINA

Opposite:
Ariene Bethea in the North
Carolina home that she shares
with her husband, Daren, and
their puppy, Mini.

ARIENE BETHEA HAS A TALENT for selecting one-of-a-kind special pieces. It serves her well in her work as an interior designer, and even more so as the owner and huntress for her successful design studio and vintage furniture shop, Dressing Rooms Interiors Studio. Her unique aesthetic and the arresting way in which she combines influences from different eras are showcased in the many layers of her Charlotte, North Carolina, home. Hiding in plain view in this treasure trove of eclectic art, colorful textiles, and furnishings of many eras is an extensive collection of heirlooms passed down from mother to daughter and grandmother to granddaughter. But Ariene's home—where she lives with her husband, Daren, and their puppy, Mini—is the story of the most important thing that her mother and grandmother passed down to her: the ability to put it all together.

Ariene's training in design and her love for vintage furnishings came more by accident than by interest. For the first five years of her life, Ariene lived in a home in Uniontown, Pennsylvania, with her maternal grandmother and uncle. Her mother lived in Washington, DC, for work and felt safer leaving her daughter with family than taking her chances on childcare in an unfamiliar city. Though design was not Ariene's interest early on, she quickly learned from her grandmother that everything has its place.

The living room is an exceptionally curated gallery of African and Asian objets d'art. African sculptures sit beside Asian ceramics in perfectly tailored vignettes.

On the living room wall, a white juju hat
from Cameroon sits in stark contrast to
an inherited mask from Indonesia.

Above:
Ariene's mother bought
the modular sofa in 1965.
Reupholstered in pink velvet,
it's now the statement piece
in the home's sitting room.

Opposite:
The home features a collection
of treasures from all over the
globe, including a variety
of African masks on the wall in
the dining room. The artistic
vignette extends to the dining
table, where a sculpture
discovered at an estate sale
lies.

"My grandmother knew where everything went," Ariene recollects. The house was her grandmother's first home after living in a housing project. "She stopped school at age ten to take care of her brothers and sisters. Then she took care of her kids. After my grandfather died from black lung, she received a check from the coal mine. So she never worked." As a result, Ariene received her undivided attention.

"I wasn't the only grandchild," she admits, "but I was the youngest. And I was spoiled because I was the only girl." Always her grandmother's helper, Ariene saw her exacting standards up close. "I would always ask if I could help water plants and clean the table, but I guess I would arrange things in a way that wasn't exact. So my grandmother would always come behind me, moving everything a couple of inches. My grandmother and my mom decorated that house together and they took a lot of pride in the home," she explains.

When she turned five, Ariene joined her mother in an apartment in Washington, DC. "That's the place I think of as home," she reflects. "It's where I spent the most time and have the fondest memories." The transition from country to city living turned out to be an easy one.

Right:
The vintage dinette set carries a lot of meaning. After inheriting it from her grandmother, Ariene had it restored and reupholstered, and it's now the center of her home office.

Black-and-white photography by South African visual artist Zanele Muholi has been used to create a graphic gallery wall in the living room.

"My grandmother was very protective," she remembers. "She didn't let me hang out with the neighborhood kids." But after moving to DC, friends were easier to find. "We were always playing at the park or going to the zoo, so I was always outside." She found that her mother and grandmother approached their decor in different ways as well.

"Nothing ever changed at my grandmother's house," Ariene remembers. "She had an owl statue at the bottom of the stairs when I was a kid. Thirty years later, after my uncle died, we went to her house and it was still there." Conversely, her mother was a seemingly endless well of design inspiration, with limitless energy for bringing her visions to life.

"She was always doing something: wallpapering cabinets, refinishing chairs, or stripping the floors. It was a lot of work, but she loved it." Though she didn't take part in any of her mother's projects, Ariene learned by osmosis as her mother crafted their environment. "I didn't realize it, but obviously that affected me subconsciously," she says.

Life fell into focus for Ariene while living in Boston. She finished graduate school there while living with her husband and college sweetheart, Daren, who was completing chiropractic college. While working after school, Ariene had the chance to decorate her boss's office, and everything changed. Design went from something that she watched to something that she did—and did well. Inspiration struck to open her own vintage shop, and she hasn't looked back since.

Boston also sparked the urge to own a home. "I'd spent most of my life living in an apartment, but my husband grew up in a house," she explains, "so we were both ready to live in a house again." With close friends leaving the city and no interest in Boston winters, the pair set their sights on North Carolina. It was a welcome transition that brought Ariene full circle with her design journey and her family story of homeownership.

"My grandmother owned her home, which was important, especially in that time, as it was our biggest form of wealth," she says. Her mother, on the other hand, never owned her apartment, despite forty years of residence. To Ariene, the choice was clear. "For me, owning signified adulthood and the whole American Dream. Something of my own that I could design my way, without limitation."

Unfettered, and with much more space to operate in, Ariene's house became a living mood board. Just as her mother's rooms before her, Ariene's rooms change constantly, caught in a ceaseless flow of ideas

> "My grandmother owned her home, which was important, especially in that time, as it was our biggest form of wealth."

and inspiration. But even more than a place for expression, the house is a repository for the designer's memories of the women whose creativity helped shape her own.

"I have my grandmother's dining set," she says with a smile. Once thought to be lost, Ariene recovered it from her uncle's estate after his passing, along with the owl from the bottom of the stairs and one other item. "There was a trunk, a theater chest that she had gotten when I was about twelve. She told me, 'I'm getting this for you and if anything happens to me, this is your chest.' I was like, 'What's gonna happen to you?'" she says, laughing.

Her grandmother's dinette set became the central point in her home office, where it provides the perfect setting for client meetings and planning sessions for the shop. "I grew up with that set, so I wanted it in the house somewhere, just not as a dinette set," she explains. "That space has changed a lot because how I work has changed." Her most treasured piece, however, is the sectional sofa that occupied the living room in the apartment she shared with her mother in Washington, DC. Though it was little more than part of the background for Ariene when she was a child, her own changing relationship to furniture and the circumstances under which she received the set helped to give her a different perspective on it. "I inherited this set when my mother passed," Ariene explains. "She bought it in 1965 on layaway, and she was always having it cleaned. I didn't get why it mattered when I was a kid. But now I understand." Each heirloom sits in the context of Ariene's own choices, but even those show influences from childhood.

"My mom loved combining African and Asian art. I didn't realize how much I mix the two until a customer told me. She was surprised by how well they went together, but that's just how I grew up." Ariene's colorful art is supplemented by her lifelong love of black-and-white photography. "When we first got the house, I was obsessed with black-and-white photography of jazz musicians." As a result, it's as easy to find classic images of Ella Fitzgerald or Charlie Parker on her walls as it is to find photos of family members.

Ariene Bethea has an eye. It mixes past and present as skillfully as it does colors and patterns because of the unique way in which she sees the elements from which she creates her rooms. Underlying Ariene's style is her belief in the power of material things—not to convey status, but to hold memories. Each piece Ariene curates from her childhood matters to her because it mattered to someone before her. That connection helps to keep present with her those who have already passed. "They tell a story that I don't have to tell," she reflects. "I'm glad I had the forethought to save so many things after my mom and grandmom passed, so those memories are always with me."

Right:
The home features an eclectic
mix of African and Asian
objects. In the bedroom,
a suzani blanket and Asian
art are mixed seamlessly with
leopard print fabrics and
noir sculptures.

MEMORIES OF HOME

Opposite:
The stairway gallery wall is
an altar, holding memories
of Ariene's mother, father and
uncle. Another frame honors
Richard Henderson, an ancestor
who aided in the Underground
Railroad.

GROWING UP, I KNEW that Richard Henderson was a family name, my uncle's name. After my mom passed, while I was sorting through her things, I found papers about another uncle named Richard Henderson who had been part of the Underground Railroad in Pennsylvania. He had been born into slavery in Maryland in 1801 and escaped by the time he was fifteen. Making his way north to Pennsylvania he eventually opened his own barbershop—a prestigious job at the time. Over the years, Richard Henderson's safe house sheltered more than five hundred people on their way to freedom, often as many as twenty at a time.

—Ariene Bethea

The Journey Home: THE GREAT MIGRATION

In the absence of slavery as a formal institution, a series of social, legal, and economic structures were erected around the Black community, ensuring that slavery would continue in effect if not in form. In 1896, the Supreme Court case *Plessy v. Ferguson* established separate but equal as legal doctrine, leading to the laws collectively known as "Jim Crow." Segregationist laws created and enforced a condition of inferiority for African Americans that was reiterated constantly in daily life. Unemployed African Americans remained at the mercy of Southern courts. Hard labor became a common sentence, with longer terms forced on anyone unable to pay court fees.

While Jim Crow ruled the South, in the North, industrialization replaced abolitionist sentiments with corporate profiteering. US Steel was one of many companies that purchased Black laborers from Southern counties. For decades, tens of thousands were "rented" by US Steel to labor in Southern coal mines. Chained in the dark, tortured, and subject to assaults by overseers and fellow prisoners alike, many were left in shallow graves or incinerated in the mines' industrial furnaces. Many more were sold to local farms and commercial interests. Courtrooms became the new auction houses for purchasing Black bodies, with the friends and supporters of judges able to obtain laborers directly from their courts.

From roughly 1910 to 1970, the Great Migration—a mass exodus of African Americans out of the South—saw some 6 million Southern Black people relocate to destinations around the country. A major catalyst of the movement was the emergence of new employment opportunities in the North and West. The outbreak of World War I in 1914 caused a gap in European immigration that left scores of American industrial jobs vacant. Desperate for labor, corporations that had previously pursued exclusively racist hiring practices, including US Steel, began actively recruiting Black laborers from the South.

New communities were created as large numbers of African Americans left the South. Previously existing enclaves across America experienced massive population booms. Once again, for African Americans, home became both a destination and a question.

Wherever African Americans migrated,

Family photos hang on the wall in the
hallway of Alexander Smalls's Harlem
interior. Images of Alexander's mother
and aunts in gold picture frames create
a regal feel.

they were greeted by segregationist policies from the government and private landowners alike. Private owners used race covenants written into ownership deeds to prohibit the sale of houses and land to Black owners or to prevent interracial housing. Municipalities issued segregationist zoning ordinances, while banks and other commercial interests instituted a practice called "redlining" to exclude predominantly Black neighborhoods from opportunities and resources, such as supermarkets, banks, and businesses, or to target them for price gouging. By convention and code, realtors were instructed not to assist African Americans with finding homes in "white" neighborhoods.

Kept out of desirable housing, Black people were forced into overcrowded and dilapidated tenements, often for much higher rents than white tenants paid. In Philadelphia, African Americans were routinely charged four to five hundred dollars more than the going rent for white tenants, with rents in West Philadelphia increasing by an average of 100 percent between 1914 and 1920. Similar practices existed in Cleveland, Detroit, and Los Angeles.

Despite the challenges, Black communities grew and thrived, responding to segregation and redlining by creating their own businesses to meet the needs of their communities. In many places the creation and survival of these neighborhoods depended largely on the activism of Black realtors, such as Andrew F. Stevens Jr., a Philadelphia-based realtor and banker who served in both the city council and city legislature. But perhaps the most pivotal such figure was Philip A. Payton Jr., the Father of Harlem.

Payton opened his real estate office in 1900, successfully lobbying white tenement owners to admit Black tenants. Eventually able to purchase his own buildings, Payton is credited with beginning Harlem's transition into a center of Black life and culture, and protecting it. When the Hudson Realty Company replaced every tenant in three Black apartment buildings with white occupants, Payton responded by purchasing two exclusively white buildings and evicting the tenants to make room for those Hudson displaced. While his business was relatively short-lived, by its end Harlem's future as the new Black center of New York City was clear, setting the stage for the Harlem Renaissance and all that followed.

In 1906, Greenwood was founded in Tulsa, Oklahoma, by O. W. Gurley, a wealthy Black landowner. Beginning with the purchase of 40 acres, Gurley built a boardinghouse and lent money to those who arrived in Greenwood wanting to start a business. Other entrepreneurs and activists, such as J. B. Stradford and newspaperman A. J. Smitherman, arrived and contributed to the growing community, which was eventually home to some ten thousand African Americans. Though not everyone in Greenwood was wealthy, the level of affluence among Black people there rivaled any other community in the nation, and far outstripped that of many of its most immediate white neighbors, leading to its moniker: Black Wall Street.

Across the country, several vibrant communities flourished under the name "Bronzeville" between the 1930s and 1950s. Perhaps the most influential was in Chicago, located on the city's famous South Side. As the early '30s saw the Harlem Renaissance draw to a close, Chicago's cultural flowering reached new heights, producing pivotal figures in music, literature, art, and academia. It was also a burgeoning economic center, boasting a wide array of businesses including the city's first Black-owned bank.

At much the same time, Milwaukee's Bronzeville was also a center of culture and economic growth and was the home to many civic and business leaders. A third Bronzeville emerged in 1942 in Los Angeles's Little Tokyo. African Americans arriving to find work in the booming war economy were restricted to neighborhoods left vacant by the internment of Japanese Americans. Overcoming early problems of overcrowding and makeshift housing, the community quickly flourished. Renowned for its energetic nightlife, Bronzeville's after-hours scene was built around jazz clubs, brothels, and breakfast clubs—bars that stayed open well into the morning. The end of the war in 1945 and the return of interned Japanese Americans to their homes brought this community to a close only three years after it began.

Though many strong Black communities emerged as a result of the Great Migration, not all fared as well as those in Harlem or Chicago. Many communities in the North and South were erased through explosions of white violence. Prior to the turn of the century, New York's affluent Seneca Village was violently raided and cleared by police, following a lengthy legal battle to make way for Central Park. In 1912, a Black community in Gainesville, Georgia, called Oscarville, was eradicated by white rioters. Nine years later, Greenwood in Tulsa was sacked in what is now one of the most infamous incidents of ethnic cleansing in recent American history.

White mobs burned homes and shot occupants as planes were used to drop incendiaries on businesses and homes. In all three instances, and many others, accusations of rape made by white women against one or more members of the Black community led to rushed trials or dubious confessions, followed by lynchings and mob violence against all African Americans in the area. Often the incidents would be deliberately forgotten, omitted from histories and schools, just as the Tulsa massacre was for decades. In other cases,

the cover-up was more literal. The remains of Oscarville in Georgia were submerged under Lake Lanier, much like many other Black communities destroyed by violence elsewhere. Zoning for highways and other "urban renewal" projects were also popular means of destroying Black communities—such as Milwaukee's Bronzeville—while leaving few traces of the community that existed.

The Great Migration carried millions of African Americans out of the South. Hoping to escape the apartheid of Jim Crow and the horrors of the South's reconstituted slave trade, they searched for new homes in distant parts of the country. Met with different versions of the same legalized oppression and threatened constantly with violence, they found a way, creating communities that would have a massive impact on the culture and politics of the nation. The spirit of these communities is perhaps best exemplified in the story of Greenwood. Just months after the massacre killed hundreds and destroyed thousands of businesses and homes, the community had rebuilt, growing stronger than before.

For all those who were zoned out, redlined, or succumbed to mob brutality during the Great Migration, even more persevered. Making homes in hostile lands, they raised their children, passing on their knowledge and strength to those who would be born generations later.

CREATIVE HOMES

Take a look inside the abodes of dancers, writers, artists, and designers. Here are the homes of the influencers whose vision and creativity help move the culture forward.

The home of John Goodman features a bright array of collected pieces, including art, textiles, and stunning sculptures.

STACEY AND ANDRE BLAKE: A LIFE IN COLOR

IT WAS MORE THAN TWELVE YEARS AGO that Stacey Blake's blog, *Design Addict Mom,* first brought the world into her Fayetteville, North Carolina, home, introducing an online audience to her children and their colorful environment. The blog, which began as a creative outlet for a first-time mom on maternity leave, invited followers to experience Stacey's love of great design, radical joy, and unprecedented color. "I love showing my home on Instagram and my blog because it shows that we're more than oppression," she says. "We're more than an oppressed people. It's important to see images of us in spaces where it's happy and it's positive."

A schoolteacher with no formal interior design training, Stacey's message of design liberation was accepted just as quickly as the images of her stunning multihued interiors. Her aesthetic, where color is embraced freely, is inspired by the Jamaican heritage and upbringing that she and her husband, Andre, share.

Stacey's life began in Kingston, Jamaica; her childhood and formative years were split between the urban landscape of Kingston and the rural area of Clarendon, where her mother's family lived. Affectionately, Stacey describes her life in Kingston as "humble." "My mom worked at least two jobs. We didn't have much, but the great thing about it is I didn't feel lacking. Home was always filled with love," she says.

Right:
This home is a story in color.
The bold blue living room
features pops of orange for
a fun and energetic vibe.

Above:
An abstract wallpaper print in shades of blue and yellow adds a dose of the Caribbean to the dining room.

Opposite:
In the entryway, Stacey's curated a gallery wall featuring some of her favorite artists, including Brooklyn Dolly, Jean Jullien, Mafalda Vasconcelos, and Suzy Lindow, against a vibrant, bubblegum pink wall.

Education was her mother's first priority for her daughter, and Stacey didn't disappoint. "I was smart back in the day," she says with a laugh. "I started high school really young, at about ten years old." But the end of elementary school also meant the end of her days in the city. She left her mother and stepfather in Kingston to attend a boarding high school near her mother's childhood home. The proximity allowed her to avoid boarding and she stayed with family instead. "I was with my grandmother," she remembers, "and I had uncles and cousins who lived just a stone's throw away."

As she would quickly realize, things worked differently out in the country. "It's two very distinct lifestyles," she explains. "Even the language and how people speak changes from region to region—still what we call patois, but the accent could be very different. I had to be very different." Coming from a farming family, she picked up a number of life skills, along with her school education. "I still grow my own food," she mentions. "Not all of it. But hopefully one day I can get to that level."

Also from Kingston, Andre left Jamaica for the United States to join the Army. After he proposed, Stacey left Jamaica to join him. Once they

In the boys' bedroom, the map behind the bed was part of a nightly ritual where the boys could spot where Daddy was while in the service; a beautiful way to keep the family close.

were married, Andre's career as a member of the Army Special Forces took the couple all around the world together, but Stacey often found herself spending a lot of time on her own. "Typically, he'd be gone for a year at a time," she recalls. "Like in Italy. Because the war in Iraq had just started, as soon as we landed there, my husband was gone." As she was navigating life in a new country and learning the language on her own, she also found an interest in interior decor.

As Stacey explains, at first it began with "just painting a wall here and there, but Italy was the catalyst." Stacey found that the furniture design of the country held a particular interest for her, not only because of its beauty but also because it reminded her of home. "Craftsmanship in Jamaica is a big thing as far as making furniture and wood pieces. Even now, I gravitate toward pieces that are so well made, they transcend time." Surrounded by some of the finest design in the world, Stacey quickly became an admirer, then a student, and finally an addict. "I was buying a lot of furniture, especially in Milan," she admits with a smile.

For Andre, Stacey's transformation wasn't hard to notice. Every time he returned from deployment or spoke with his wife over video chat, she had transformed their home. "It was a little maddening at first," he says with a smile. "I would come back from work and the dining room would be in a different place. Or you're expecting a living room and there's nothing there. Sometimes I'd be like, 'Where's the couch?'"

But despite not knowing quite what to expect every time he opened the door, Andre was Stacey's first and biggest fan. "I knew it was important," he explains. "She was expressing herself and it gave her something positive she could focus on, just being creative in her space." It became even more important when the couple returned to the US and came to their current home.

The vibrance of the couple's North Carolina home is stunning. Stacey credits her culture and upbringing for her embrace of vibrant hues. "Jamaican culture is just colorful," she says. "There was no distinction from country living to city living. We're just a vibrant people."

Every element speaks to the family's Jamaican roots. The home opens on a deep pink entryway, offering a refreshingly energetic backdrop to the gallery of paintings that adorn the wall. Through an archway, one of Stacey's favorite architectural features of the home, a lively shade of blue takes over the walls. It's broken up by splashes of orange from the sofa and the trio of sliding wooden panels that cover portions of the bookshelf.

"Jamaican culture is just colorful. There was no distinction from country living to city living. We're just a vibrant people."

Opposite, top:
It was important to Stacey
that Cheyenne have art in her
room that represented positive
images of Black women. The
piece by French graphic artist
Aurélia Durand adds a special
dose of Black girl magic.

Opposite, bottom:
Cheyenne's bedroom is a mix
of candy-coated hues. The
abstract wallpaper in every
shade of the rainbow provides
a colorful backdrop.

A formal dining room that originally found life as a playroom for her sons, Zion and Ian, has grown with the family. Now a chic and stylish space in its own right, its neutral-toned walls offer a brief moment of stillness in a whirlwind of bright shades. Accented with beautifully patterned pieces, the dining room features a large chalkboard wall where Andre draws art for the children.

Much of the design of the home keeps the children in mind, offering them space to play, dream, and explore. When Andre was in the service, Stacey applied her skills as a teacher and a designer, using a massive map of the world to create a feature wall in the boys' bedroom. Every night before bed they could find exactly where Daddy was on the map and wish him a good night.

For the littlest Blake, Cheyenne, her room is a world of color, supported by the many hues of the wallpaper that cover one side of her bedroom and the bright orange feature wall that highlights the space near her bed. Between the two, a glittery tent offers escape to countless other worlds of imagination and fun. And in the main bedroom, Stacey painted the walls a bright shade of coral to energize the space. Complementary art continues the color story, and plants and textiles add to it as well.

Admittedly, the sunroom is Stacey's favorite space in the home. Blessed with huge amounts of daily sunlight, it's the natural place to show off the majority of her amazing collection of plants, a fond reminder of life in Jamaica. There are more than thirty in the home, and Glory, the massive fiddle leaf fig, is a feature all her own. Stacey's enormous prized plant has even gained an Instagram audience that follows her adventures on the @Glorythefig feed.

"When you're used to an environment, you don't really notice it," Stacey observes. "I grew up with a lot of plants but I was just born into it. I don't want to say I didn't appreciate it, but it's definitely refreshing when I go back to Jamaica to visit." Now, for Stacey and Andre, having plants around for their kids is part of their effort to give their children some of the culture that they grew up with while preparing them for the world that they're growing up in.

"I always joke that we have our own subculture at home," Stacey remarks. "Along with our colors and plants, we also tell the Anansi stories that Andre and I grew up with." It's an important life lesson for her children, not only in design, but also in making home a sanctuary from some of the harsh realities she faced when she first arrived in the United States.

"I guess I went through a reality check, so to speak, moving here and living this life and then having children," she reflects. "I didn't realize how great the line of demarcation between Black and white

Above:
In the family room, a chair from Albany Park is covered in an African wax print pattern, a nod to the family's African Diaspora culture.

Opposite:
The family room is home to Stacey and Andre's fourth child: Glory the Fig. The giant tree has been in their family for more than a decade now.

is. In Jamaica, we have all different colors and it's not something we necessarily experience until we come here. It's just a sad reality."

For the last nine years of their more than twenty-year relationship, Stacey and Andre Blake have made their home an oasis of color and culture. And while she loves sharing glimpses of her ever-evolving interior with the world, Stacey is clear that her priority is the space she's able to create for her children and what they can take from it to learn and grow.

"I want them to have good memories," Stacey says, thinking of her children's futures, "impactful ones that will last into their adulthoods. When they think of home, I want them to think of a loving environment, a place where they can be themselves, express themselves. Most of all, a safe place." A true teacher at heart, Stacey is just as conscious of what her blog can give to those who follow it. "It's important for others to see that how we live is not just what they see on TV," she reflects. "And it's important to remind our community that, despite everything, despite the inequities outside of your home, inside you can still cultivate joy."

MEMORIES OF HOME

Above:
Stacey curated a gallery wall in the boys' bedroom, filled with positive imagery and messages, including "it's cool to be kind."

Opposite:
Stacey and Andre's coral bedroom feels like a Jamaican sunset. The room features a selection of art, including an "Only Love" pennant from rayo & honey.

MY MOTHER WAS RENTING until she built her own home, which she now owns. I would say she had a layperson's point of view as far as building, but she reached out to her circle. When I lived in Jamaica, people didn't usually have access to architects. It was usually that you knew someone who knew someone, you're familiar with a carpenter, you have a friend who's a builder or a handyman. And so it's almost like a family collaboration. And it takes time. Someone will have a great idea to start building and they'll start gathering materials. But the budget is often a concern, so that may slow the process down some before they're able to continue. It can take as much as a year, but she figured it out and she got it done. And I think a lot of that rubbed off on me.

—Stacey Blake

COLETTE SHELTON: AND WHAT WE CAN, WE PASS ON

FOR YEARS, COLETTE SHELTON has had the best of both worlds. A well-placed executive at one of the most recognizable names in entertainment, she was also the mind behind one of the first and most successful interior design blogs, *Cococozy*. When, at the beginning of 2019, she finally stepped away from the executive desk, it was a moment of coming full circle. After years of pressing against her industry's well-known glass ceiling, she finally decided to go around it to create a path of her own.

When Colette was born, her parents were already well on their way to giving her a better life than they'd had to that point. When they met, both were students at UCLA. Her mother had just immigrated from Haiti, while her father was a second-generation Californian whose parents migrated from Texas in the 1940s. When Colette was born, the couple was married and living in student housing with their first child, Colette's older sister.

The first thing Colette remembers about life is school supplies. "I remember a lot of studying and yellow legal pads all over the tables," she says, smiling. "The housing we lived in was like an apartment for married students. Everyone was probably in their early twenties." A simple two-bedroom home, the space consisted of a living room with a separate kitchen and a small dining room. "All my life, before I went

Right:
Neutral elements create a
sophisticated living room.
Sofas in linen and stucco
walls make for a calming
environment.

Above:
The main bedroom is inspired by the natural splendor surrounding the home. On the gallery wall plant life, architectural details, and brass leaves are on display, an ode to California living.

Opposite:
Colette uses color as a way to delineate space in her home. A nook painted in deep blue becomes a library where you can rest and read a good book.

to college, I grew up having dinner every night, with my parents," she says.

Though student housing didn't afford much opportunity for decorating, elements of style and culture nevertheless found their way into the home. "There were all these little touches of where my mom grew up," she reflects. "She kind of structured our living space and she had pieces like the dolls my sister and I would play with, or a little wooden sculpture of a couple kissing that she had brought from Haiti. We had these things we called Haitian boxes. I don't even know what they were for. But there was always a Haitian box on their dresser where they kept jewelry or little items."

It was time spent with family that Colette remembers most about growing up. "We spent a lot of time at my grandparents' house—my dad's mom and dad. We were there a lot because my parents were at school and my grandmother would often babysit and take care of us." Time spent with grandmom meant hearing stories about life for her family before California. "My great-grandfather was an emancipated slave," Colette remembers. "And my grandfather was a groundskeeper

Opposite:
In this cozy dining room, the
eye is pulled up to the blue
ceiling, which feels like
you're looking at the sky.

for a country club before they left." The stories painted the picture of a much different world than the one Colette was growing up in. "She would tell me about this happy life that she had with her parents and three sisters, but at the same time there were all these poignant moments of racism and the strength they had to have at those times."

In one such story, Colette's grandmother awoke late one night to find her cousin, Romy, frantic. "He'd been at the local store and somebody accused him of looking at a white woman," Colette relates. "And just like that he had to go on the run. The whole family came to my great-grandparents' house in fear. Romy had to run all the way to Kansas." Later his family would sneak onto a train to escape as well. "My grandmother remembered that night, how terrified she was, how everyone was sobbing. And they never saw them again. There's a whole wing of my family that continued in Kansas that I don't know because someone said that Romy looked at a white woman. That was all it took to change our lives."

With extended family on both sides all throughout Los Angeles, family gatherings were frequent and festive. "On my dad's side all the entertaining happened at my grandmother's house. And then a lot of my aunts and uncles also lived in the area. My mother grew up with nine brothers and sisters and four or five of them were in LA. So we all got together on the weekends. We would go to my aunt's house for the big Haitian party and we had this trove of cousins to play with. It was really wonderful," she remembers.

One of the best things an extended, pan-Diasporic family brought to Colette's home growing up was a deep and varied library of music. "My parents liked a lot of jazz. A lot of Nina Simone and blues. But there was Haitian music as well. It was a great mixture." Music was a constant feature of the home and something that Colette remembers sharing with her father as well. "I vividly remember our record collection. The first album that my dad got my sister and me was Stevie Wonder's *Songs in the Key of Life*. We were so excited. Music was part of what made that home feel so warm. I felt protected."

By the time she was ten, life for the family had begun to change. Moving on from UCLA, her father went to Loyola for a law degree while her mother remained at the school for her PhD in French. "My mother was teaching at UCLA, but then she got a position as a French professor in Claremont, so we moved there." There was a marked difference between life in UCLA's student housing with frequent visits to grandmom's house in South Central and life in Claremont. "It was very suburban," she remarks, "and completely different. Not only were we out of an apartment and into a house, but we were also one of very few Black families in that area. It was a happy, wonderful time for me. But now, realizing what was probably happening back then . . . there were some very startling experiences," she observes. "I used to go to my best friend's house, and I was not allowed to go inside their house because her dad was racist. I don't even think I told my parents because I knew that they wouldn't have let me be friends with her."

Notwithstanding the exigencies of growing up in a mostly white, suburban neighborhood, Colette looks back fondly on Claremont, which she regards as her hometown, both for the person it helped her become and the ways in which it represents what her parents wanted for her. "My parents were extremely focused on academics and education because they wanted us to have a better life," she says. "Especially my father. He was very aware of race, and the things that happened to him growing up, and he had a very clear vision of what he wanted for us, just like his parents had a very clear vision of what they wanted for their four kids."

Colette would have her first brush with design while pursuing a degree in art history at Wellesley College. "I can't say that there was an inclination toward design," she admits. "But when I got to college I finally got my own space. It was like, 'Oh, now I get to do what I want to do.' College was actually where I started to think about my space and what it says about me."

Colette's path would then take her to law school. "My dad passed away from a heart attack around the time that I graduated from law school," she recalls. "He was fit and athletic, but, if I'm honest, like a lot of African American men, I think it was the strain of being Black in America. But he left us in a position where he knew that we were set up to be able to take care of ourselves," she explains. "It's as if he was able to leave and say, 'I put all the pillars in place so that these girls will be safe.'" One of those pillars had always been a good education. Owning a home was another.

"Homeownership was also really important to them—especially for my sister and me," she confirms. "My dad's family had one piece of land. They bought it when they got to LA. There were two houses, and both were for our family. My grandparents and their kids lived in the front house and my aunt and uncle lived in the back. They didn't have much money, but they knew they needed to buy land and they figured out a way to get it creatively." It was important for her and her sister to continue the family legacy. "My sister bought a house at twenty-nine, and I bought a house at thirty-one. My parents were so focused on it for us, I think, because they always wanted to make sure that we had a certain amount of independence, and that we were taken care of."

For twenty years, following law school, Colette enjoyed a career in entertainment marketing. After she transitioned into marketing, a

friend and business coach quietly warned her that it was often a glass-ceiling position in the industry. It turned out that she was right. Stuck with a high-paying job but no creative outlet, Colette was searching, and that search led her to design.

She stepped away from marketing for good in 2019 to focus full time on her flourishing lifestyle brand. Colette's Beverly Hills home bears all the marks of her success in both industries. It's a beautiful sanctuary where lush gardens overlook a stunning vista of the city. The Spanish-style architecture of the home offers a variety of delightful features, including spaciously appointed outdoor areas, complete with iron gates, concrete passageways, and classically tiled roofs. Inside, each room has been lovingly curated with a mix of vintage details that fit seamlessly with a ubiquitously serene palette of white, blue, and a collection of earth tones.

Pieces designed by Colette punctuate the interior. From her line of textiles to luxury serving boards, her love of design can be recognized everywhere throughout the home. In the living room, exposed wooden beams overhang a cozy seating area across from a dark blue alcove displaying books and small boxes—a nod to the Haitian boxes she grew up with as a girl. In the dining room, a farmhouse dining table is paired with Louis XVI chairs. A vintage pierced Moroccan chandelier hangs above the vignette, and the space is completed with an abstract painting in an ocean of blues.

Framed remembrances dot the walls throughout the home, standing out most in the guest bedroom. There framed pieces combine with brass floral sculptures to create a whimsical gallery wall. Colette's main bedroom is equal parts coastal retreat and expansive reading nook with rows of books adorning built-in shelves, perfect for those few days that she can spend relaxing at home.

Marrying her media background with her love of home decor, Colette produced a fifteen-episode documentary around her renovation of another 1920s Spanish-style home that she purchased in View Park, a rapidly gentrifying neighborhood that was once a posh African American enclave during the 1950s and '60s. Continuing the tradition that has kept their family moving forward since arriving in California, her sister purchased the house once the renovations were complete. "She kept everything pristine," Colette says, laughing. "They left all of their furniture at their old house, and moved in."

Home, whether as an asset or an industry, has been key to the success of Colette's family since the Great Migration, and she is quick to

> ## "Music was part of what made that home feel so warm. I felt protected."

Above:
In the dining room, the outdoors have been brought in with floral sketches framed and hung on the wall and flowers freshly picked from the garden. An abstract piece, a housewarming gift from artist Sarah Robarts, evokes feelings of being by the sea.

recognize its importance for African Americans as well as the obstacles that exist. "When we look at this whole idea of the wealth gap, I think that homeownership is extremely important," she says. "But it's difficult if you don't have family wealth. I am very fortunate. My mom helped me with the down payment on my first house after my father passed. Before that my parents helped my sister with her first house. I know that homeownership rates might be low for us right now, but I think the awareness of the need for it might be getting higher. I see a lot of young people recognizing the importance of having a piece of real estate that will give your family the resources that they need, if only to have a place of safety."

Like so many families during the Great Migration, Colette's grandparents left the South for the West with one goal in mind: a better life for themselves and a brighter future for their children. Later, her mother took a very similar journey from Haiti to the United States, with similar goals. Though her grandparents and her father are no longer with her, she has fulfilled their legacy, building upon what they left behind.

NANA YAA ASARE BOADU: SPIRITUALITY AND MOVEMENT

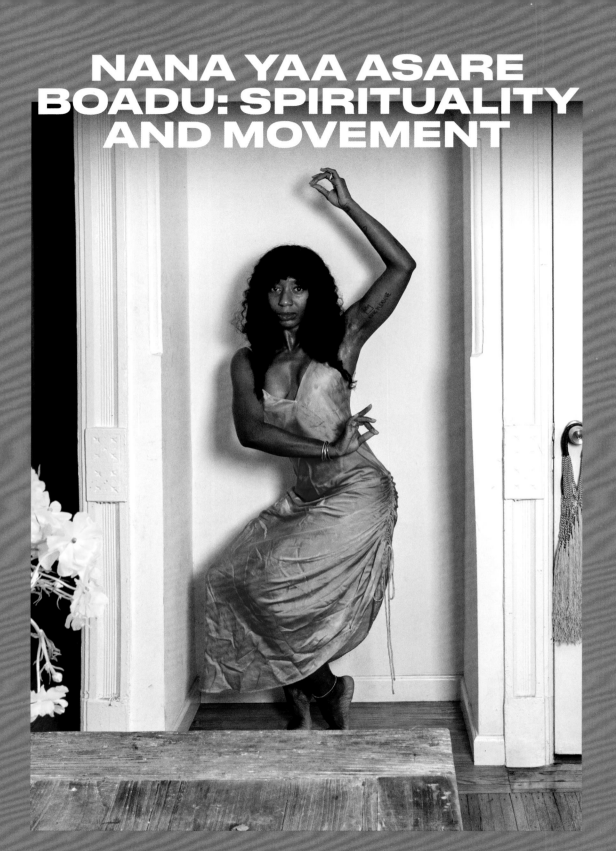

MOVEMENT IS A CONSTANT IN LIFE. Time passes and things change, and as we go we acquire pieces of ourselves, shuffling and rearranging them as we work to find the person we are and the place we can call home. For fashion designer and performance artist Nana Yaa Asare Boadu, movement is more than an inevitability: It's a necessity. As she puts it, "The only time I know who I am is when I move."

For Nana Yaa, home has been a lot of places. Her heritage and her heart are Ghanaian. She was born in London, and, since leaving England, has lived in places around the world, including Paris, Los Angeles, Israel, Milan, and the Netherlands. Now living bicoastally between New York and LA, her Brooklyn brownstone apartment is a statement on the story so far, filled with the promise of things to come.

The first place Nana Yaa ever called home was a two-level Victorian in London owned by her mother. Dividing the home by level, her mother would frequently rent out the lower half, and when the family moved to Milton Keynes, they would rent the entire house. "But when it was empty, I always used to play downstairs with friends," she remembers. "And I distinctly remember having a really amazing surprise birthday party there." As she recalls, it was one party of many.

"My parents used to throw a lot of parties. And I remember watching all these beautiful grown-ups, beautiful Black people come in and dance

Right:
In the dining room, the
architectural details have
been painted to truly shine
in the space. An industrial
dining table and chairs
complete the quiet tableau.

Above:
The bedroom is painted in the home's signature palette—an elegant off-white that creates a calming retreat feel.

Opposite:
The home is a minimalist environment where the artist can truly focus on her work—movement and designing fashion.

and laugh and enjoy the music." But no matter who came and went at the house, the center of Nana Yaa's attention was always her mom.

The daughter of a Ghanaian diplomat, Nana Yaa's mother had grown up in places around the world. "My grandfather was an ambassador for Ghana to Israel so my mother lived there for a few years learning Hebrew," she explains. "Then he was ambassador in China for a time. But then, at a certain point, he sent her and her siblings to boarding school in England with a British family." After school, her mother became an interpreter for Scotland Yard, but she still retains fond memories of the country. "She says it was the happiest time of her childhood because they were allowed to do anything,"

For Nana Yaa's family, homeownership was a foregone conclusion. "My grandfather owned a lot of homes all over Ghana," she offers, "and when my mom moved out on her own, she bought her own home as well. She's owned every house we've ever lived in. It was just our way of thinking." So it's been a break from tradition that in all her years on the move, Nana Yaa has never owned a home. "I guess because I've always moved around, I've never really thought about owning a home," she

Right:
A velvet pink sofa from Saba
Italia adds color and texture
to the living room.

considers. "But I have to say that I've been extremely blessed with every apartment that I've lived in. In every country, the right place just sort of came to me." Her home in Brooklyn was no exception.

How Nana Yaa found her place in Brooklyn is a story that every New Yorker would love to tell—because it never happens to anyone. Finding an apartment in the city is next to impossible on the best of days. To find one on your first try while living in another country is simply unthinkable.

"I was very lucky," she says demurely, "because I was in London at the time, looking for apartments on a website." Even she thought it was too good to be true. But when she sent a friend to take a look, the response was emphatic. "She was like, 'Nana Yaa, get it!'" she says, laughing. Before she knew it, Nana Yaa had a Brooklyn apartment. From there, there was one more surprise waiting. "When I finally got here, I was like, 'Oh God, it's a duplex.'"

Embracing her good fortune, Nana Yaa set about cultivating her New York habitat. The result is an intriguing paradox. Sophisticated yet lived in, curated but effortless, it's a perfect Parisian pied-à-terre in the heart of Brooklyn. Every detail is considered, but nothing is obsessed over, and every moment has a story to tell.

"I remember watching all these beautiful grown-ups, beautiful Black people come in and dance and laugh and enjoy the music."

Nana Yaa's home is full of heirlooms, but many of them aren't hers—at least not originally. "The house came with a lot of things that I just kind of inherited," she says with a laugh. One of the most intriguing is an antique scuba helmet that she keeps as a statement piece by the door. "It's just such an interesting piece," she reflects. "I mean, who has a scuba diving hat in their house?"

But small curiosities weren't the only presents she found when she moved in. The dining table, which serves as the room's central feature, was also a gift from the previous tenant.

Some of Nana Yaa's most pivotal furnishings were provided as gifts soon after she moved in. At the center of her stylishly laid-back living room is a gorgeous pink velvet sofa. The room's main pop of color, it easily beats out the fireplace mantel as the primary attention-grabber. It completes the scene so perfectly that it feels like the rest of the space was designed around it. But its arrival was more serendipitous.

"I have this amazing friend who has a furniture company in Milan," the designer relates, "and she told me, 'You should have a pink sofa.'" Though a dusty pink wasn't her first thought for her living room color palette, upon seeing the gift, Nana Yaa was convinced. "I thought, 'Why not? It kind of goes with the house.'"

Stacks of books, the designer's sketches,
and collected sculptures create a
tranquil vignette in the corner of the
living room.

At ten years old, Nana Yaa left London and her mother to live in Holland. "My mom was having to travel a lot for work," she remembers, "so she gave me the choice of going to boarding school in Ghana or moving to Holland for two years to stay with my favorite auntie and uncle." Having seen the discipline at Ghanaian boarding schools firsthand, Nana Yaa didn't find it hard to choose.

Two years turned into ten. Nana Yaa grew up in Holland with her aunt's family. Like her mother in the English countryside, she quickly found that she was one of the few people of color and the only Black girl.

"London was way more multicultural," she reflects. "I never thought about my skin color until I went to Holland. Then it became, 'Oh, I'm a Black girl,' and realizing that Black was the first thing people saw." It was a shift that she credits with awakening her own cultural curiosities and sense of self.

"I became very interested in what it is to be Black," she says, "because all I knew was that I was always the only Black girl and the way I was treated didn't seem right." Creatively, she looked for ways to express this identity. As a child, she clipped images from her aunt's magazine collection that then became her own Black fashion magazine. Later she painted and played sports as she went through a teenage tomboy phase, learning to use her athletic body while coming to understand her own beauty and the context in which that beauty was developing. While the move to Holland brought about a certain awakening, it was also a moment for Nana Yaa to consider what she'd lost.

"Growing up, my mom took me to Ghana every year until I was ten years old. So it's just always been part of me. When I moved to Holland with my aunt, it was a very Dutch upbringing, about as far away from Ghana as I could imagine. We never went to Ghana. We never spoke Twi at home. Eventually, I lost the language. When I returned to London in my twenties, I went to Ghana and I remembered. Seeing my family again, just being on the continent, it brought everything back. And I remembered how great it was growing up with Ghana as part of me without even thinking about it." Yet the start of Nana Yaa's journey back to London and then Ghana would come not through her fascination with culture but through couture.

Fashion was always an interest for Nana Yaa, but it was never a career goal. "I was always obsessed with shoes and clothing," she admits. "As a child, I would sit at the dining table drawing whole collections for my dolls." It wasn't until a classmate's suggestion to check out an art school that the door to fashion opened—and opened wide.

"I went for this interview at an art academy," she begins, "and I put together everything that I had done over the years, even my drawings from when I was six years old." It wasn't hard to gauge their reaction.

Nana Yaa was admitted on the spot. Suddenly, she was a fashion designer, and it was fashion that would lead her back to London for school, then Paris and Milan for work, before sending her to New York.

Just as the years have seen Nana Yaa occupy many homes in several countries, her creativity, too, has moved and evolved, changing form and format as she searches for her truest means of expression. One day, that search caused her to simply start moving. Without words or any formal training in dance, led only by emotion and a sense of where the universe was taking her, Nana Yaa's body began to express all of the things that she had no interest in saying. The result was explosive.

All it took was Instagram, and Nana Yaa's new expression—equal parts dance, performance, and confession—became a sensation. And a shy little girl, who wanted to edit magazines and then created fashions, became a performer, a choreographer, and an influencer. "When I move," she postulates, "it's about the story of the body. As soon as I put on a piece of clothing, that informs my movement, it informs the energy."

Like her movement, Nana Yaa's home is a form of expression in small gestures: The little touches that complete the space also mark it as her own. Since she was young, books were the only presents she ever asked for. Now they take up more space in her apartment than any other object, except perhaps for shoes. Arranged into statuesque towers of varying height, books sit like cairns around the edges of each room, topped with small sculptures, old cameras, and other curiosities.

Like the books, shoes act as decorative touches in just about every room. On the stairs, a series of platform heels point the way to the second floor. At the top, a row of sneakers sits stylishly atop a stool. In the dining room, two pairs of heels hang from a stool topped with a short stack of books. Of course there's also a shoe library in the hallway-sized walk-through closet between her living room and bedroom.

Movement, for Nana Yaa, is as much a metaphor as it is an expression. In moving she acquires space, without asking permission or offering apology, far beyond any gaze that might accuse or affirm her in any way. It seems like exactly where she's always wanted to be. But if someone is always moving, how can they ever feel at home?

"I need to have a place which is completely mine," she intones. "And it's kind of dawned on me that it all just goes back to Ghana. I need to be there. It gives me something that no other place in the world can give me. That feeling that's just like, 'Oh, I'm home.'"

Opposite:
Designer John Goodman in his
condo in the Bronx.

JOHN GOODMAN'S HOME is a testament to many things: his love of objects, his need to be surrounded by vibrant colors, and a deep sense of maximalism, for a start. But there's more. For John, filling his home with interesting things isn't about boxing himself in; it's about finding space to get everything that's inside of him out.

Born to a young mother, John grew up living with his grandparents in a single-family home in the Bronx. "I was basically raised by my grandparents," he explains. "We had a nice front yard and a backyard. My grandfather would plant collard greens and all kinds of different vegetables."

Living as sharecroppers in South Carolina before migrating north in the 1970s, John's grandparents had a well-established facility with growing, and John had an attraction to things that grew. The garden was a world that drew him in immediately. "A plant will become a flower on the way to becoming a vegetable. But I was always fascinated by the flower portion of it. Even a flowering squash, when you look at it, is a beautiful flower," he muses. "As a kid I would pop off the flowers and make little floral arrangements for Barbie dolls and GI Joes." The garden was the foundation of his bond with his grandfather. But the rest of his attention was reserved for his grandmother.

"I think it was her style," he considers. Like the flowers in the garden,

Right:
In his condo, John has carved
out multiple spaces for living
and entertaining. Blue carpet
is used as a colorful divider
between the living room and
dining area.

Opposite:
John has amassed a large
collection of African
masks over the past decade.
Above the sofa, a few of his
favorites are on display.

John was drawn to the glitter of his grandmother's outfits. "I was intrigued by the elements and the layering of it," he says. It was a style that extended to her home through her love of hunting for antiques.

"She would find flea markets, estates, anything," he explains. John was her constant companion on trips that ranged far and wide, looking for anything new—trips that showed him far more than furniture. "We would go to sales at homes in the Hamptons and Connecticut, and I would see how they lived. It just opened me up." With each trip his notion of the world expanded, along with his ideas on who he could be within it and what he could call his own. "Coming from the South Bronx, you don't see those things," he says. "We would always find amazing pieces to bring back to the house. And we'd just display them all over the place."

Today, John's home showcases all the benefits of his early experiences with his grandmother and grandfather. John creates new worlds of his own using pieces from his ever-evolving collection of curiosities, art, and rare finds. In each room of his home the result is a highly curated experience—an artistic endeavor to be discovered, studied, and enjoyed.

Growing up, the same broad sense of style was all around him. "My grandparents' house was eclectic," he says with a smile. "There were a lot of different things going on. The style was a mix of Hollywood Regency, a little bit of '70s and some '80s as well." In every room there was an emphasis on keeping things nice, but one room was especially sacred. "The first room came before the living room," he remembers. "And the first room was like, 'You just walk through, you don't touch anything.'"

By the time he was fourteen, John, his mother, and his two brothers had moved from his grandparents' home into a nearby housing project. It was a hard transition. As is true for many Black families, his grandparents' home had been the unofficial center of life for his extended family. "My grandmother cooked every day. And on Saturdays all my aunts and uncles would come over and we would have a huge dinner. Fun times, good music, dance," he says. "That house just felt like love."

After the move it was a different story. Where his childhood memories were full of the outdoors and exploration, his teenage years were spent inside. "It was really a rough area," he reflects. "And I wasn't made for it at all. So I really wouldn't go outside because I just didn't feel like I was part of that environment." Without his grandfather's garden or his grandmother's antiquing trips, John's world grew smaller. And for the first time his understanding of himself didn't seem to fit within the space provided by his surroundings.

Spending most of his time inside, John's creative leanings found new expression through art. "My mom took me to art classes at the Bronx

Museum of the Arts," he explains. "There were amazing artists from around the world who would come to teach. I started with watercolors and just evolved from there."

His evolution led from painting to drawing to fashion, taking him to New York's High School of Fashion Industries and then college at the Fashion Institute of Technology. "I was drawing garments," he says, "but I wanted to be able to make the garment. So I started taking pattern making. That's where I really started getting a lot more creative."

Though an artist at heart, John would land a job in technology after school, working with computers at Goldman Sachs. The position would allow him to help his mother and eventually buy a condo. "I stayed with my mom at first so that I could take care of everything," he says. "She was able to finish high school and go to college. Now she's a nurse."

Once he had a place of his own, John began collecting things to fill it with. "I started collecting African art while I was at Goldman," John explains. "Every pay period, I would buy African masks. I currently have about seventy of them," he says with a laugh. "I am a collector. I'll take anything that I can find. It can be a sculpture, a painting, it could be a pencil, as long as it has a silhouette or something I can connect to."

> "I can do paintings. I can do planting. I do everything. And I want to be everything all at once."

This wide-ranging aesthetic is evident in his work today as a floral and event designer, and in his interior as well. John's collections have become so large that he has multiple storage units holding the items that won't fit in the condo. Meanwhile, at home, the visuals change so often that visitors a week apart might have completely different experiences. Still, there are some things that can always be counted on: A mix of bright hues is a must, along with a multitude of objets d'art on display. Stunning floral designs can be seen everywhere, weaving houseplants into artwork, while bold displays and visionary designs express the world as he sees it. Though his early career took him in the direction of technology over art, it was John's time working in an office that led him to design.

"People knew I had a fashion and design background," he explains, "so they would come to me to throw a party or a Bar Mitzvah, and I would create great events for them." After the crash in 2008 and the Great Recession that followed, with its disproportionate impact on Black workers, John was out of work and options. "I was applying for jobs and no one was hiring. I found a company that was hiring for seasonal Christmas design. I went in understanding that the position was only for two months. When they saw what I could do, they hired me full time to manage the floral department. That's how I got back into design," he says.

After studies in horticulture and apprenticeships under some of New York's best in floral arranging and event design, he found that he could do more with flowers than make them look good on a table—he could tell stories and create new worlds. "When I create a space or a table or an arrangement, I want you to be drawn into it," he offers. "I like things that stimulate your eye. So I try to find pieces that do that. It's like a conversation but played out visually." Combining bright visuals with eye-catching and unexpected objects allows John to be artist and curator all at once. While he's more comfortable combining the two roles than choosing between them, the only difficulty John finds is when people's admiration of his creations conflicts with their assumptions about who could have created it.

"I designed an event one time," he remembers. "And I'm the only Black person in the space. Everyone's looking at one of my pieces and admiring it, saying how amazing it is, but I'm standing next to it, completely unseen." The experience was not new to John. Even as a child, people had a hard time connecting him with his art because it didn't fit their image of what a Black kid from the Bronx could be. And even now, as he combs through his collections at his storage units, there are puzzled stares or awkward questions from those he encounters. "They usually assume that I'm working for someone who owns the unit," he says, rolling his eyes. "When they realize that I'm the owner, they get very confused, as if they can't imagine how I got all of this."

Whether in his grandfather's garden, his room in his mother's apartment, or now in his own place, home has always been where John can create without limitation and without explanation. The maximalism that seems to define his home is rooted in a search that has gone on since his first flower squash, his first look at a Connecticut estate. It's a search for the creative space to be who he is—all that he is—and for others to see him and all Black people as we really are. "We do everything," he says plainly. "I can do paintings. I can do planting. I do everything. And I want to be everything all at once. I just want whatever I do to be acknowledged and seen and understood by everyone, because Black people are not one thing."

MEMORIES OF HOME

Above:
On the coffee table sits one of John's favorite pieces: an African woman carving by a Nigerian artist.

Opposite:
In the dining room, John has crafted a chair out of his collection of Kermit the Frog plush dolls.

TRACING BACK MY FAMILY'S history, we don't know what part of Africa we originate from, but we know that we were purchased by the Goodman family in South Carolina. The plantation house is still there, although it is falling apart. My great-great-great-grandfather was actually able to purchase land from the master. So we know where the family was enslaved, and, at one point, we owned a total of 120 acres. Unfortunately, a lot of it was broken up once my grandmother and her sisters passed away. But before my grandmother passed away, she put 15 acres of land in my name. So even now, we still go back and we know where we came from.

—John Goodman

The Journey Home:
FROM THE GREAT DEPRESSION TO THE GREAT RECESSION

Between the Great Depression and the signing of the 1968 Civil Rights Act, strategies for disenfranchising would-be African American homeowners had developed considerably. Not only were African Americans disproportionately hit by the joblessness and homelessness of the Depression, New Deal funds intended to restore the nation were also famously lopsided in their allocation. Starting in 1934, the Federal Housing Administration pursued a deeply segregationist national policy, providing millions in funds for middle- and lower-income white families to secure suburban homes, while African Americans were refused loans and ushered into urban housing complexes. Southern states manipulated categories to exclude sharecroppers and other agricultural workers—the majority of whom were Black— from receiving unemployment benefits. The racist distortion of programs alleged to benefit Americans regardless of race would continue long after the Depression had passed.

The GI Bill, arguably the primary mechanism for building the American middle class after World War II, has a similar history of discrimination. Despite supposedly having equal access to the program, Black veterans had benefits routinely denied or altered from what their white counterparts received following their service. The disparity was especially apparent in housing.

As early as 1947, *Ebony* magazine reported that of 3,229 VA housing loans awarded across 13 cities in Mississippi, only 2 went to Black veterans. Moreover, the VA adopted the racist policies of the Federal Housing Authority, restricting Black families from using GI Bill– insured loans to purchase homes in newly expanding suburban vistas, such as Daly City or any of the Levittown enclaves being built by Abraham Levitt and his sons. And while African American veterans were being denied the right to live in new suburban developments, new developments in America's cities were destroying the communities they already had.

Like race covenants and redlining, zoning laws have long been used to prevent African Americans from owning homes in desirable areas or to destabilize existing Black communities. Following the 1949 Housing Act, the nationwide initiative of "urban renewal" offered billions in federal funds for

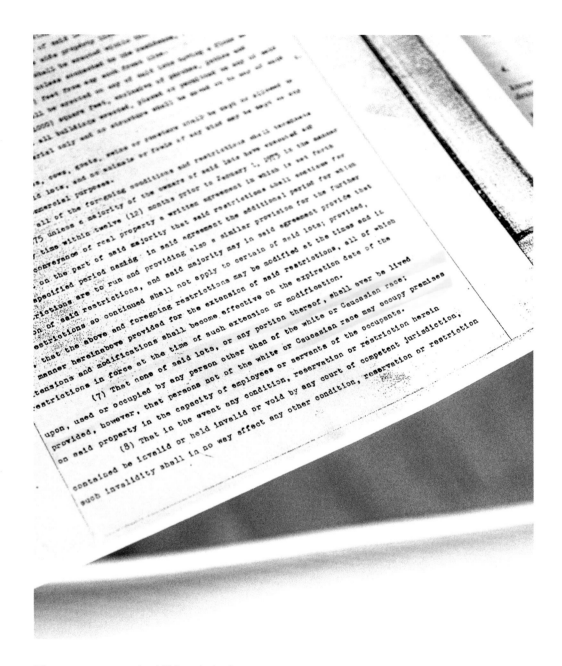

The race covenant still exists in
the contract Treci and Amir Smith
signed when purchasing their home
in Bonita, California.

cities to target, clear, and redevelop or sell areas considered "blighted." As generations of discriminatory housing and employment practices had ensured that the most impoverished parts of any American city would have mostly, if not entirely, Black populations, it's no wonder that author James Baldwin famously referred to the initiative as "Negro Removal." By 1956, more than 300,000 families, as many as two-thirds of them people of color, were displaced by federal renewal programs alone, to say nothing of state-driven efforts.

Additional displacements were funded by the passing of the 1956 Federal Aid Highway Act, which built the nation's interstate highway system. While connecting the nation's major cities, through the construction of 41,000 miles of highway, the act also demolished the communities of color through which those roadways were directed. Whether through urban renewal or highway construction, those who owned homes and refused to sell risked having them taken under the policy of "eminent domain," a practice that continues to reinforce gentrification efforts today.

By 1976, more than 1 million Americans had been displaced by the highway system as well as through continued renewal projects. Though most were people of color, many were not. However, even the process of losing a home differed significantly between Black and white displaced communities. Where white residents were directed toward homeownership opportunities, Black displaced residents were ushered to public housing or the rental market. The process further entrenched a system of generational wealth disparity already hundreds of years in the making. Yet an equally long tradition of activist movements by African Americans was having an impact as well.

On April 11, 1968, the Fair Housing Act was signed into law as Title VIII of a second Civil Rights Act. The title built on the Civil Rights Act of 1964 by specifically outlawing race covenants, redlining, and other forms of institutional discrimination that had, for generations, worked to disenfranchise African Americans seeking to buy property or homes. By the time it was signed, however, America was a nation in crisis.

Martin Luther King Jr. was killed in Memphis, Tennessee, seven days before the Fair Housing Act was passed. In the shadow of the outrage that poured out of Black communities in cities across the nation, a previously indifferent Congress passed the law, spurred on by President Lyndon Johnson. A little more than a month after the signing, three thousand people would begin living in tents on the National Mall ahead of a march of fifty thousand to protest the ongoing conditions of poverty in the country, specifically in the areas of income and housing—and in fulfillment of the slain visionary's last dream.

Resurrection City was the forward arm of the Poor People's Campaign, a march designed to bring together impoverished Americans of all colors to demand better treatment from their government than they'd received from Johnson's "War on Poverty." Led by Ralph Abernathy following Dr. King's assassination, the tent city endured harsh conditions, but together with the passing of the Fair Housing Act constituted a fitting tribute to the life and work of Martin Luther King Jr.

Built on the recommendations of the Kerner Commission, which warned that America was becoming "two nations, separate and unequal," the Fair Housing Act was a landmark piece of legislation. It continued the upward trend of African American homeownership that had been going on since the late 1940s through its peak in the late '80s. However, despite its intentions, the legislation that was passed—the third iteration of the bill—contained significant concessions, particularly concerning enforcement of its policies, that severely mitigated its overall impact.

The act went into effect under President Richard Nixon, who appointed political rival George Romney as secretary of Housing and Urban Development (HUD). Despite his good intentions, Romney was consistently stifled in his efforts to remove what he referred to as the "white noose" of American housing policies from the collective necks of Black communities. He pushed consistently for housing integration, particularly in the suburbs, which remained stubbornly closed to Black and Hispanic buyers. Outright opposed by state governments and suburban communities, and undermined by the Nixon administration, Romney failed at nearly every turn, resigning from the position after Nixon's reelection in 1972.

As a result, though outlawed by the Fair Housing Act, redlining and other discriminatory practices have remained widespread within the banking and real estate industries. Studies conducted in 2015 show that nearly 30 percent of mortgage applications submitted by African Americans were denied that year. Yet that number represented a significant improvement from the 45 percent of Black applicants who were refused in 2000.

Prior to 2000, African American homebuyers were already frequent targets for subprime loans. From 1993 to 1998, the number of subprime home loans awarded in the US increased by 900 percent, with 39 percent of high-income Black homeowners receiving subprime mortgages, as opposed to 18 percent of low-income white homeowners and only 6 percent of high-income white homeowners— and that was before the boom of 2003 to 2007.

The repeal of certain banking regulations in 1999 led to the creation of a new group of high-risk financial products with confusing and often predatory terms. Like earlier types of subprime loans, these were primarily offered to Black and Brown homebuyers. Because they were often presented as refinance options, the high default rate made them as effective for foreclosing on existing customers who already owned homes as they were for selling new customers houses they could not keep. Cities with large Black communities, like Cleveland, Ohio, became the nation's largest markets for subprime mortgages. At the height of the crisis, as many as one out of every ten homes in Cleveland had been repossessed.

Leading to the stock market crash of 2008, the subprime mortgage crisis was the highlight of the Great Recession that began in 2007 and lasted until 2009. While America suffered as a whole after the crash, much like in 1930, Black and Brown households took the brunt of the collapse. Between 2005 and 2009, the median wealth of African American households dropped 53 percent compared to only 17 percent for white households. The gap in homeownership between Black and white college graduates has only widened since the recession and, as of 2019, average rates of wealth still lopsidedly favor white households at a rate of 10 to 1—$17,000 to $171,000— irrespective of education.

African American homeownership rose to new heights in the decades following the passing of the Fair Housing Act. Yet the persistence of racist lending and real estate practices led to an economic collapse that, in turn, served only to widen the gap of wealth and homeownership between Black and white households in America. Today, the rate of Black homeownership has fallen to levels not seen since before the Fair Housing Act was passed— and that was before COVID-19. But shining new light on the broken parts of history offers us a chance to build anew.

BOSS HOMES

The homes of entrepreneurs, executives, and shot callers, these are the spaces of those whose talents and hard work have transformed them into their own brands.

The main bedroom in Rachel and Dediako Rodgers's home features the family's growing art collection, including a piece by Canadian artist Gordon Shadrach in the seating area.

RACHEL AND DEDIAKO RODGERS: HOME ON THE RANCH

GREENSBORO, NORTH CAROLINA

RACHEL RODGERS, HER HUSBAND, DEDIAKO, and their three children are living the dream, occupying a 57-acre ranch in Greensboro, North Carolina. Complete with horses, the "Rodgers Ranch" is a sprawling estate owned by the former lawyer from Queens who has always been in search of space.

The property, which is about one square mile, has been a place for Rachel and her family to establish not only space to live and grow, but also a design aesthetic that supports the family's cultural heritage. The family collects Black art to feature in the home, with pieces by today's most sought-after artists, including Ronald Jackson and Gordon Shadrach. In Rachel's office, Sheila Bridges's Harlem Toile de Jouy covers the back wall. And in one of her daughter's rooms, a Black butterfly wallpaper makes a statement of African American beauty. "I want my children to grow up in a space where they see themselves reflected," says Rachel.

Growing up in Flushing, Queens, in a small apartment, Rachel shared the one bedroom with her older sister, while her parents slept in the living area. Apartment life was familiar to her parents. "Both of my parents grew up in Queens," she explains. "My mom's family is Irish and lived in a housing complex that was created for workers in the electricians' union. That was the only way you could get in, and her

The blue sectional in the family room
is a nod to the sectional that Rachel
enjoyed as a child at her aunt's house.
Now, with one in her own home, it's a
place where her children can relax and
enjoy life.

The living room is absolutely perfect for the family of five, with lots of space to enjoy. Above the vast fireplace sits a piece by acclaimed artist Ronald Jackson.

The dining room is a beautiful play of blues, pinks, and shades of purple. A silver foil wallpaper, Equis, is perfect for the ranch, which is home to several horses.

dad was part of the union." Her father, originally from South Carolina, grew up in the city as well. "He's the oldest of nine kids but [his] mom passed away when he was pretty young. After that his father moved up to New York."

While the apartment was small, for Rachel, she still looks back on it fondly. "It felt big to me," she reminisces, "because I was little. I felt we had tall ceilings, lots of molding. It was just home, and it was comfortable because it was familiar." Family friends could be found on almost every floor in what was a tight-knit community. "Summer nights, everyone would just hang out. People would set up chairs out front or sit on the stoop. The kids would play and run back and forth across the street. And that was the best. That home was filled with more people than with furniture," she muses. "My uncle and my aunts used to come and babysit us. Different family members would stay with us at different times. And I just felt loved. I felt supported in my home."

On the other side of the street from her building were a number of single-family houses. "We just assumed that they had money because they lived in houses instead of apartments." At that age, very few of Rachel's friends or relations had houses of their own, and the homes across the street stood out.

"My aunt Shelley was the only person I remember who owned a house. And that was such a big deal. She had this basement den where the kids could hang out and this big, beautiful sectional. And I remember loving that we could all sit. All the family and the cousins and stuff. And I've wanted that in every single place I've ever had. I want a gathering space for family and friends to be together because that's what fills a home with love."

The family eventually moved into a larger space to accommodate everyone. "My mom got a job working as an admin for Columbia Artists," she reports. "And my dad became a peace officer at a hospital on Roosevelt Island. They bought a condo in a really nice building on Forty-Fifth Avenue where we spent most of our childhood."

Growing up, Rachel's group of friends was very diverse, as fit the tone of the neighborhood. "It was very multicultural," she reflects. "And that was celebrated. We had an international food night, and we'd all bring food from our families. Everyone was represented: Nepal, India, China, Korea. My little group of friends included people from Germany and Korea along with my Black friends from the US and Trinidad. It was beautiful. And I think it made me really want to travel."

As a young girl, Rachel settled on law as her profession, inspired by the lawyers she saw on TV. "My mom used to watch a lot of courtroom

"I get to watch my son ride his horse on his ranch and that's pretty dope."

Opposite:
Rachel's office is designed
with client meetings in mind.
A large sectional and plush
chairs create a cozy and
inviting environment.

dramas," she remembers. "There was always a lawyer advocating for the little guy. And I used to watch that and be like, 'That's me. That's my role.'"

In college she would intern for Hillary Clinton, and during that time she learned valuable lessons that would set her on her professional path. "The legal counsel was a Black woman," Rachel recalls, "and she would bring me everywhere. She would take me to the cafeteria for lunch and introduce me to everybody." Looking back, she realizes that these were more than simple gestures. "She was opening doors for me." Something that Rachel does today in her own business, which helps Black women attain financial independence and grow wealth.

Returning to New York for law school, she met her husband, Dediako, a Brooklyn native with a brownstone in the city. "It was always under construction," she says with a laugh, remembering the home. "He was renovating, and it seemed like it was never done. We didn't have a kitchen. The bedroom was pretty much the only thing that was finished." Eventually, they needed more and bought their very first house in New Jersey.

"We had an apartment first," she says, "and then we bought a house," an 1,100-square-foot cottage that they purchased just after eloping. For her and Dediako, this was the moment they could start building a home for themselves. "My husband made us a dining room table," she says, smiling. "I think that's the first time we started to try to make our home a little bit more comfortable. We still have it."

After law school, she struggled with finding a place in the usual corporate law structure. Eventually, she decided to go in a different direction. Moving into the niche of virtual law, she soon found herself with a healthy roster of clients, many of whom were women entrepreneurs. In addition to legal advice, Rachel found that many of her clients were turning to her for business advice. "Clients would ask how I was making so much money. And that was kind of news to me, because I have a lot of kids, I had a team to pay, and I still felt like I was struggling." But the conversations led to an epiphany, which led to a new approach.

Keeping the same base clientele of women of color entrepreneurs, Rachel's focus shifted from legal services to business coaching and soon turned to wealth building. "My first foray into it was really about helping women entrepreneurs make more money in their businesses. But there are obviously gaps between white women and Black women because we're not getting bank loans. Our friends and family don't have the money to be our first round of fund-raising." She had a desire to teach women to build their businesses as she had.

With a new business, and three children, the couple was looking

Opposite, top:
Riley's bedroom is fit for a
princess. The space includes
pieces that reflect the
family's African American
heritage, including Butterfly
wallpaper from AphroChic.

Opposite, bottom:
The main bedroom is a relaxing
oasis for Rachel and Dediako
in the home's signature
palette of lilac and blue.

for more space. Before long, Rachel and Dediako were expanding their search to other states. "After looking for months, we decided to research places where Black people make up a large portion of the middle class. Every city was in the South." A friend suggested they look at North Carolina. "We came down to check it out. And we were immediately like, 'Done.'" Two years after moving, the family was living in the house that they had built, the home Rachel believed was their forever home, but then a 57-acre ranch appeared on the market and everything changed.

Originally the plan was not to become ranchers. "The company spends a lot on event venues every year," she explains. "So we were actually imagining a place where we could host retreats." Once they saw it, there was no question about whether they would buy it. "Within five minutes of walking onto the property, my husband said in my ear, 'This is a must-do.'" Still believing it was a business expansion, Rachel had no objections. "Then the pandemic happened. And I remember lying in the yard at our old house and thinking, 'We should just buy that house and live in it.'"

For the little girl inside, the one who grew up sharing bedrooms in apartment complexes filled with family, having nearly 60 acres for her family was beyond amazing. "Space is one of the big things for sure," she muses. "And light. I hate dark, small spaces. We had a big room in the first apartment we lived in, but it was pretty dark, and the condo I grew up in had a ton of windows that brought in a lot of light." Her new home is light-filled and also filled to the brim with pieces that support the new life she and Dediako are building for themselves and their children. "It feels amazing," she says with a grin. "I mean, I get to watch my son ride his horse on his ranch and that's pretty dope." The only problem this new home poses is figuring out what to do with all the space. "I've never had a formal and an informal dining room. Much less a formal living room and another living room. That's a lot of couches," she says, laughing.

JASON REYNOLDS: LIFE BETWEEN PAST AND FUTURE

WASHINGTON, DC

LIKE THE REST OF US, Jason Reynolds lives in the present. But his approach to it may be somewhat more intentional than ours. More than anything else, Jason sees the present as the bridge that connects the past and the future, and he always seems to have them both in view.

Every time he leaves his house, Jason passes a slip of paper hanging in a frame on the wall—a rejection letter his grandmother once received after failing to qualify for a cleaning job because she couldn't pass the written test. Jason framed the setback as a reminder of the importance of the work he does, why he's leaving the house, and why he needs to come back.

To say that Jason works with words might be understating the facts. He's a best-selling author with a host of awards to his credit, having written more than a dozen books for teens and young adults. His commitment to helping younger generations forge their own relationships with the written word is palpable, real, and wholly unintended. It's a focus that starts in the past, with the loss of his grandmother.

As a boy, Jason's relationship to reading and writing was simple: They didn't get along. All that changed when he was ten years old. His grandmother passed, and he saw the impact that it had on his mother. "It's the first time I ever heard my mother cry. I didn't see it. Because my

Right:
On the home's top floor, a
modern lounge is perfect
for entertaining. A collection
of photographs by Maurice
Pellosh hangs above the custom
blue leather banquette.

Above:
The gallery wall in the living room features the works of numerous Black artists, including Jamilla Okubo, Christopher Myers, Artemio, and Marcus Leslie Singleton.

Opposite:
In the living room, a quilt by Bisa Butler is framed and hangs above the sofa.

mother was the sort of strong Black woman that we wish they didn't always have to be. But I could hear it through the wall and it was, like, chemically changing." His desperation to help his mother feel better turned an enemy into an ally, and he penned a six-line poem that his mother printed on the back of the funeral program. "That was the moment everything changed," he remembers. "But it was never about me. It was always about service. How can I change the temperature of a room? How can I stop my mother's tears?"

A pass through Jason's home won't reveal many mementos of his mother, but there's a reason for that. "I don't fool with my mother's stuff," he says. "She lives around the corner. I'm always in that house." What it will reveal is a deep attachment to color. A dedicated advocate for his readership, especially those most at risk, Jason spends a lot of his time visiting schools and juvenile detention centers—two worlds that share a common color scheme. "I spend my whole life in institutions," he reflects. "I'm in schools. I'm in prisons. Places that are typically black, white, and steel. I can't feel like that when I come home."

Intentionally set against a neutral backdrop, color enters every room

The bedroom features Jason's love of midcentury modern furnishings and more of his burgeoning art collection. Pieces by Jamilla Okubo, Christopher Myers, Artemio, and Marcus Leslie Singleton hang on the wall.

on different levels and through different means. The white walls of his open-plan living area are broken up by an explosion of yellow from a brightly hued accent wall intended to enhance the room's daily dose of natural sunlight. In the same space, which includes the kitchen and bar areas, numerous other shades make their presences felt in equally dramatic, albeit smaller, bursts.

In his bedroom and office, located on separate floors, things become serene almost to the point of austerity. In the bedroom, the blazes of color that cover the hall recede into a meditatively hued room, distinguished by the lightly patterned, neutral-toned wallpaper. Pops of blue from the table lamps, an apricot-colored chair, and a few scattered moments of color are all that remain. In the office, the white walls reappear. Inspiring the clear mind it takes to create characters and shape their lives, the wall's color is reflected in the room's one chair, while yellow and blue make their appearances through the rug and file cabinet. It's a house full of bold color choices and the expert pairing of seemingly random pieces. And while it doesn't include any specific pieces from his mother's house, Jason will be the first to confirm that the concept behind his home is all her.

> "There have to be books in every room in my house, and I keep books in certain spaces for certain reasons."

"Mom has always had really interesting tastes," Jason reflects. "Our house had Rodin replicas and a huge Buddha." A longtime student of Eastern thought and meditation, Jason's mother kept a meditation space in the laundry room for daily use. But Buddha and Rodin weren't her only design influences. Music was a presence as well. "There was a piano, a pipe organ, and an upright piano in one house—and an old trumpet with a little clip just kind of attached to the wall. I don't know how she pulled it off because we were not those people. But that's the kind of stuff I think about more than anything."

Now in his own home, Jason's creative spirit benefits from being surrounded by the things he needs most: his books and his art.

"I'm a huge collector," he says, beaming, speaking about the works scattered throughout his home. "I have been for a long time." Art can be found in every room of the house, from a variety of sources. In his living room, a gallery wall intended to class up the television includes a piece by Afro-surrealist Alim Smith, framed in pink. Another favorite, by Adebunmi Gbadebo, is prized for the statement it creates using Black people's hair. "Hair is hard for Black folks because of all the things that get attached or encoded into it," he offers. "But it's something that connects us, all of our genetics, everywhere in the world. We should be praising it."

Books are perhaps the only thing easier to find in Jason's home than works of art. "There have to be books in every room in my house, and I keep books in certain spaces for certain reasons." Art books stay close at hand on the sofa and in the bedroom because they're small and easy to pick up. Literature in the office is a source of inspiration and reference. His collection exceeds the confines of bookshelves in the living room and office to find homes on nearly every flat surface of the home. But the abundance of books is more than an image requirement for the author. It's an artist's relationship to his art and how he sees the work he does in the world. "It's almost like spellcasting, what I get to do for a living," he muses. "All I've got is twenty-six letters. That's my whole toolkit. Twenty-six letters that I somehow have to arrange and rearrange into some intricate code that chemically changes a person. And so I keep my tools around."

The author began using those tools with purpose for his first published work, a coauthored fusion of poetry and art for teens. "I never wanted to write novels," he confesses. "I wanted to be Langston Hughes." But when a friend later convinced him to give it a shot, he found that the only people he could show what he had created, "a book about Black kids hanging out in Brooklyn, being Black," were editors in the young adult category. It was his first major success, titled *When I Was the Greatest*. Since then Jason has not only come to embrace his medium and his audience, but also to see in the connection between the two a vital part of his own experience and a crucial opportunity to help.

For Jason Reynolds, the past and future are key ingredients of the present. The former gives it context, while the latter gives it purpose. In the same frame that holds his grandmother's rejection letter, Jason keeps all the contents of her wallet, including her voter registration card, both symbols, he says, of her perseverance. In his office, he keeps an Ernie-shaped Sesame Street cookie jar belonging to his grandfather, one of the few frivolities of an austere life, together with artifacts of African American literature, including letters from Langston Hughes and an autographed first edition of Toni Morrison's *Beloved*. He has designed his home so that the past is always in front of him—and so is the future. Fueled by his own experience and that of his family, Jason works to reach those intentionally designated as unreachable, a process he likens to the way a voice shatters glass by holding its resonant frequency. "This is what I'm most passionate about," he concludes. "All I'm really trying to do in my work is be honest about who I am, who I've been, and then figuring out how to bend my version of honesty into contemporary tone. And then sustain it. And it breaks the glass of a young person every single time."

MEMORIES OF HOME

Above:
On the bookshelf, important tomes by many of Jason's favorite authors are on display, including a first edition of *A Dialogue* by James Baldwin and Nikki Giovanni.

Opposite:
At the entryway, Jason has framed the contents of his grandmother's wallet—her voter registration card, union identification card, medical ID, and a rejection letter she received—as a way to honor her legacy and the one he continues to build for his family.

MY GRANDFATHER INHERITED 200 acres of land from his grandfather. So he never had to ask for anything, and in fact white people had to ask him for some things. Because of that, my mother didn't know that she was living in the hotbed of Jim Crow. When she was little she could go to the ice cream shop and tell the white lady behind the counter to give her whatever she wanted and her daddy would pay for it later. But the ice cream lady didn't insist that she keep every spoon she used to be nice, but because no white person could be expected to use a spoon once my mother's lips had touched it. Black people today have a lot of things against us, but perspective is important. I tell young people all the time, "If you feel like your life is hard, ask your grandma to tell you a story. You'll find out that you alright."

—Jason Reynolds

BRIDGID COULTER: DESIGNING SANCTUARY

BRIDGID COULTER HAS ALWAYS HAD AN EYE for detail. Even now, she remembers nearly everything about her childhood home in Berkeley, California. "It was just unique," she muses. "There was a big porch with huge wide stairs leading up to a side porch and inside the beams were stained a dark mahogany. I remember the fireplace having a very ornate iron grate and a tall mantel that I couldn't see over. I was so happy when I was finally able to look into the mirror over the mantel."

Her attention to detail has served her well. It's been an integral part of building her career as an actor, an interior designer, and an entrepreneur. She's had equal success in building a family, raising two children with her husband, actor Don Cheadle. It's with a meticulous eye, in every endeavor, that she works to carve out a space that she can safely call her own. Looking back over her journey so far, she puts it plainly, "I was always looking for sanctuary," she says. Now, in her family getaway in Hawaii, she has finally found it.

The island retreat that the family calls home part of the year, in a bicoastal life between California and Hawaii, is a chic oasis designed completely by Bridgid. Within cream walls and high A-frame ceilings, the home is filled with a mix of contemporary and artisan details. Art that the couple has collected over the years is featured in the house. Two commissioned paintings of Queen Liliuokalani and her brother,

Right:
In the main bedroom, a graphic grasscloth wallpaper and shell lamps are a reminder of the sea that's just feet from the house.

Above:
In the living room,
a collection of blue batik
pillows reflects the
ocean vibe of the home.

Opposite:
The family enjoys playing
games together, and some
of their favorites are on
display, including this
handmade chess set.

James Kaliokalani, hang in the living room in recognition of Hawaii's history and native heritage. A mix of print and pattern added in gives a nod to Bridgid's California style.

Bridgid's family arrived in California long before she was born. Her mother's side hails originally from Marksville, Louisiana, where her grandfather was a traveling blues musician. He came from a musical family: His cousin was the famous harmonica player Little Walter, and his band, which included Bridgid's grandmother, toured California frequently. "They got invited to do some of the blues festivals," Bridgid explains. "So they made their way to California. It was kind of a gold rush for music, and they pursued that while working regular jobs to support the family." Eventually, they settled there permanently. Growing up, Bridgid could always find them—they lived in a nearly identical house, right across the street from hers. "They basically co-raised us," she remembers.

Comparing and contrasting her house with her grandmother's led to some important revelations for Bridgid early on. She quickly found that she felt differently in different spaces, influenced by colors

and layouts on a level that affected not only her mood but also her thoughts. "Dark mahogany is really distinct and interesting," she says of her childhood home, "but in a small house, it's really deep. So I had all these deep, pensive thoughts." Her grandmother, however, loved bright, open spaces. What was dark brown in her parents' house was a creamy white at her grandparents'. "It was definitely a respite," she says. Reflecting on the dichotomy, she could see the role both played in her formation. "There was something about our house that was comforting, and sometimes looming, and then at my grandmother's house was freedom. It was the mix of all the things that made me who I am, and I'm grateful for it."

A child of the 1970s Bay Area, Bridgid recalls the conflicting emotions of the time. "It was a complicated childhood," she admits. "There was this mix—a kind of stress, tough times, and the dreaminess of being a flower child." One source of the family's stress was negotiating life as an interracial couple with children. "It was really intense," she recalls. "I don't even know if my parents' marriage was legal at the time it happened."

The family home was cozy, though maybe slightly cramped for a family of five. This led Bridgid toward exploring the expanses within herself. "I started making movies in my mind," she reminisces. For a while, this inward focus only added to her shy nature. Then she discovered acting, and the stage, and found a way out of her shell. "I geared myself toward loving performing arts because you could understand the human condition and drop into these characters."

At the same time that she was discovering theater, Bridgid was discovering design as well. Realizing her connection with spaces led to a fascination that began to coalesce very early. "From about twelve years old, I started drawing out the floor plan of our house," she says, laughing. The kitchen especially was an area of interest. "I kept drawing out the kitchen because I knew something just wasn't flowing right." In college at UCLA, when she got her first apartment, everything changed. "It was just dreamy," she swoons. "My own space. A whole studio apartment. And I could do whatever I wanted with it." Bridgid became a fixture at flea markets and garage sales. "There was always some piece of broken furniture that I was for sure going to fix," she notes with a smile. "About 50 percent of the time I did not." Broken or not, furniture was constantly being placed, repositioned, and replaced as new finds usurped the old.

For most people, acting and design would seem to have very little in common, but for Bridgid there was a relationship between the two. "The connection," she remarks, "is in creativity. Seeing a blank space or a lot of land and being able to see the potential, creating a world on a blank sheet of paper or an authentic human experience from words in a script."

Regardless of the medium, collaboration is one of the key components of creativity. So when Bridgid found the person she would spend her life with, sanctuary became a thing that they would build together. "We first started dating right out of college," she remembers. "So in a way we've grown up together in our adult lives, and our stories of home have blended." As she and Don set about the process of blending their stories, it helped that the narratives already held a number of compatibilities— aspects that weren't identical but close enough to allow easy recognition and the development of a shared notion of what felt right. "His sense of home is definitely Midwestern," she says with a laugh. "And my family's from the South. But what united us was authenticity. Our families are all real, authentic people. So there was no pretense with either of us. If you go to his parents' house, they're playing spades. And in my house, we played poker, war, and dominoes." This common ground proved invaluable as the couple worked to create new definitions of home. "It helped us to know how we wanted to build a home, our family, and to have some sense of regularity."

Looking into their home today, nods to that sense of authenticity are everywhere. The home's white walls echo the creamy shade that Bridgid found so soothing at her grandparents' house, while the wood details are an homage to the dark wood walls of the home she grew up in. And in the living room, a chess set and a guitar in the corner speak to cherished family traditions: game nights, music, and time spent together.

With both of their acting careers on the rise, Bridgid and Don found it difficult to maintain the sense of regularity they'd worked to cultivate. The tumultuous combination of travel, press commitments, and shoots on location left both of them with little time to spend at home. By 2005, Bridgid was ready for a change. "I didn't want a nanny raising my kids," she says. "I decided I would only do guest spots and local stuff that wouldn't really affect me raising them." The transition also opened up opportunities for a new career pursuing an old passion. After three years of courses at UCLA, she entered a new world as an interior designer.

Because design is not an industry in which African Americans are typically represented, it's a difficult space for a Black woman to be seen. "I got to this particular place in my career where I had a sense of success," she remarks, "and I didn't see us in it. And that's a lonely

> "If you go to his parents' house, they're playing spades. And in my house, we played poker, war, and dominoes."

Above:
The main bathroom has a spa-like feel in restful neutral tones with a deep soaking tub.

Opposite:
A simple corner nook pops with the addition of a leather side chair in a deep red hue. African and indigenous artworks mixed into the wall decor continue the cultural story of the home.

feeling." Bridgid was convinced that something needed to be done to change the situation.

That conviction eventually became a new venture—Blackbird, a coworking space developed by Bridgid for Black entrepreneurs. "I want us to find each other," she reflects, "to have a real shot at equity. Because it's harder for us to be seen and too easy for us to be rejected; to be called too 'tribal,' too 'coastal,' too 'ethnic.' We have to have a place where we can look out for each other, because we know that, in most places, there's no leadership that's gonna protect us."

When Bridgid Coulter was a child, she wanted a space where she could be herself. At first, all she could do was imagine it. Later, she found it on the stage and in front of the camera. When she had a home to call her own, the possibilities multiplied. "I could do whatever I wanted," she says. "I was always experimenting with how to make my space as much of a sanctuary as I could because it was mine." Her home in Hawaii is that childhood dream realized, a tropical sanctuary where she and her family are free to be themselves.

MEMORIES OF HOME

Above:
A painting above the credenza speaks to indigenous Hawaiian culture, something the family deeply respects and honors.

Opposite:
The circular dining room at the center of the home is perfect for intimate family dinners.

OWNING HOMES HAS always been important for both of our families. My husband's family owns a number of houses in Kansas City, Missouri. My grandparents inherited our first family plot in Marksville, Louisiana. Then they started buying the lots next to them. And we still own them all. And when my grandparents came to California, they knew to buy immediately. I don't know how they did it. As a Black person in California in the early 1960s, you could only buy in certain neighborhoods.

Tracing our history back to that first plot of land takes us all the way back to our arrival in the US—to the first two members of our family here. Those first two had maybe fifteen kids, and then the kids had kids and so on. So there's a lot of history, a lot of family members and cousins. It's so big, we're on like a five-thousand-person Facebook group. I don't know most of them, honestly, but it's just amazing.

—Bridgid Coulter

DANIELLE BROOKS AND DENNIS GELIN: THE DIASPORA AT HOME

DANIELLE BROOKS IS ONE of Hollywood's more recognizable faces. The star of *Orange Is the New Black*; multiple plays, including *The Color Purple* and *Much Ado About Nothing*; as well as a stirring biopic of the iconic Mahalia Jackson, Danielle is a talent who will be enriching our culture for years to come. But none of that matters when she goes home. At home, she's "Danny," either the first or second "D" in the playful "D&D" moniker that she shares with her husband, Dennis Gelin. And to Freeya, their beautiful two-year-old daughter, she's Mom.

No matter where she lives or where she goes, in her heart and soul Danielle Brooks is a country girl. Born and raised in South Carolina's Upcountry, her memories of home begin with the huge, billowing tree that stood in front of her house and a path by a small creek that led about a mile through the woods to the neighborhood park. "I remember going down that path with my younger brother on our bikes and being a little scared," she says with a laugh, "because there were so many animals around and we were always looking for snakes."

Danielle remembers life inside the home as being warm and beautiful and filled with people. Despite having little extended family around, the home never lacked for guests. "We were the only Brooks there," Danielle remembers. "Everybody else was scattered around different states. So our church members became our family. We would

Right:
This home is an ode to color,
with crisp blue walls, golden
drapery, and green velvet
sofas. The patterns, colors,
and artworks speak to
different aspects of Danielle
and Dennis's respective
cultures.

Above:
In the bedroom, a pair of
juju hats from AphroChic are
displayed over the bed. The
Cameroonian-style hats are
handmade in Danielle's native
South Carolina.

Opposite:
In the living room, pieces
by Australian artist Brent
Rosenberg are an homage to
Danielle's Southern roots and
Dennis's Haitian roots.

have all these different families for Thanksgiving and potlucks. We'd grill and play games in the backyard. Home was a safe place and it was definitely filled with a lot of love."

Those warm memories of the past have spurred Danielle to explore some of the gaps in her own family history. "I know probably as far back as my great-great-grandmother, but I don't know her name. During the pandemic my great-aunt on my mother's side told us about how her mother's property was stolen by the Klan. They had built this home for their family, purchased it with their hard work, and the Klan just came and took it. And there was nothing that they could do about it. And it shook me to know how powerless they felt. And so that is the search that I'm on right now. To know more about where we come from because that was a part that was stolen from me."

Dennis's story is, in many ways, the opposite of Danielle's. A city boy, New York born and bred, his Haitian roots stretch back through his parents to the island and to generations of extended family—those who live there and those who are buried there. "It was heartbreaking," he says of visiting the family crypt for the first time to bury his father.

The built-in shelving features
Danielle's book collection, mixed
among artistic elements, including
collages by artist Deborah Roberts.

Morbid but beautiful, the extensive catacombs hold nearly his entire lineage, and Dennis recognizes the rarity of having so much family history in one place. "I felt blessed that the family wants to keep every single person together. Even family members that pass away in the US will typically ask to be buried in Haiti with the rest of the family."

With both parents arriving in America before he was born, Dennis's connections to New York are equally strong. Brooklyn is his hometown, but it's very different from the Brooklyn he remembers. "It's kind of amazing just to see how it's changed now," he reflects. "I remember, when I was a kid, my brother was a DJ and his friends lived in Fort Greene. He would keep me in the car and just have me lock the doors like, 'You don't want to come out.'" Even so, for Dennis, growing up in Brooklyn was all about family.

"I remember my father's house was a four-family home. He was the first one to come into the country, and as he was working, he was steadily bringing family members over—my uncle, my aunts, and everybody. We had so much fun in that house," he remembers, grinning. "The block knew everybody. So if we were down the block doing stuff, they'd be like an extension of our family members. They'd watch us, tell us when it was time to go home. We would be outside 'til one or two o'clock in the morning just playing, pretty much every summer. There were so many great memories in that house on that block."

"I want her to know the safe haven that bringing positive energy into your space creates."

In their first home, a four-story Brooklyn new build, Danielle and Dennis needed space for all of their collected memories and all of the new ones that they are making together. "Building a home together has been a lot of fun," Danielle says. "Dennis has been very open to the adventure." But taking that journey together meant more than blending their tastes; it meant including touchstones of the worlds that made them—not mementos or heirlooms necessarily, but things that felt like home. For help they turned to AphroChic for our design brand's specialty of representing culture in design.

The living room is a perfect example of what we refer to as "multivalent design," in which the same elements can evoke different feelings or memories for different people. The primary colors of the room, deep green and gold against a light blue wall, were chosen to evoke feelings of nature, grass and trees, and the sky at dawn or dusk. Both Dennis and Danielle connected to the colors immediately. Danielle was reminded of the wooded path to the park behind her home, while Dennis saw the landscapes of Haiti where he spent summers as a child. Similarly, the designs on the rug and throw pillows bear a

Opposite, top:
Dennis's Brooklyn cap is a
shout-out to the city he grew
up in. A custom piece by Ronni
Nicole Robinson features
pressed flowers in concrete.

Opposite, bottom:
In the dining room, Kuba print
drapery speaks to the family's
African Diaspora heritage.

slight resemblance to *vevès*, important religious symbols in Haiti and America.

The art in the living room makes the statement most clearly. The two women depicted in a pair of images wearing head wraps could each be from Haiti or South Carolina—or anywhere else in the Diaspora. The core of this multivalent design is a recognition of the shared aspects of culture that hold the African Diaspora together, and for Danielle and Dennis's home, the understanding that the space is not about the difference in their backstories but about everything that they share together.

Much of the art they found themselves when they first moved in, including a beaded bust on the living room credenza and the wooden shield that hangs in the dining room. "We got that from the African market together," Danielle remembers. "I think it was the first purchase that we made for the house." More symbolic moments are woven into the design of the dining room. The window treatments sport a decorative pattern, similar to African Kuba prints. And the large fiddle leaf fig evokes more than just Haiti's predominantly tropical landscape and the huge tree of Danielle's memory. Originating in West Africa, the plant represents the major source of the Diaspora to which the couple and their respective cultures belong.

With so much symbolism on the first floor of the home, the upstairs is designed more with relaxation in mind. The main bedroom, conceived in a classic black-and-white color palette, is a place not just to unwind but also to luxuriate. The patterned rug continues the *vevè*-esque theme. Meanwhile, over the bed, a pair of juju hats, commissioned by a Cameroonian artisan who lives in South Carolina, is a nod to Danielle's roots.

It's a beautiful home to share and an ideal place for raising Freeya, whom the couple has promised will always have a foot in both worlds. "If she walks around with a Haitian accent, I'll be happy," Dennis beams. "I'll be happy as long as she knows the culture." Danielle also looks at the home with an eye toward the story that her daughter will write there, and what she'll carry forward. "I want her to know the safe haven that bringing positive energy into your space creates," she reflects. "When she's starting to build a home with someone, I want her to remember the love between her parents so she knows what to accept and what not to accept." Ultimately, the couple's hope for their daughter is the same as for their home—not to be two places amalgamated, but one and whole.

The Journey Home: 2020, AN UNPRECEDENTED YEAR

The year 2020 was the start of a perfect storm of natural disasters, worldwide protests, and a global pandemic that tore across the globe in a way that hadn't been seen in more than a century. Worldwide, an estimated 15 million people died from COVID-19 between 2020 and 2021. Amid the pain, panic, and suffering of widespread illness, the economic disruptions the pandemic caused around the world constituted a second disaster, as millions lost their jobs and businesses. Again, America's communities of color faced many of the greatest struggles stemming from COVID-19—struggles that are ongoing.

Even before the pandemic hit, the outlook for Black Americans was at best a mixed bag. The number of Black college graduates had nearly doubled since 1990, but Black households headed by college graduates still held less wealth, on average, than white households headed by high school dropouts. Incarceration rates for Black people were trending downward, but remained almost six times that of white Americans and there were still deep disparities in sentencing practices and treatment at every level of the legal system.

And as the Black community was still reeling from the effects of the Great Recession—more than a decade had passed—the unemployment rate for Black Americans was still twice what it was for white Americans. With regard to homeownership, which had been the crux of the financial crisis, the gap between the number of white and Black homeowners was worse than it had been in 1934, with only 42 percent of Black Americans owning their own homes as opposed to 72 percent of white Americans.

It wasn't far into the COVID-19 crisis when reports began appearing of the uneven rates of infection, hospitalization, and fatality breaking along racial lines in America. Among the groups most affected, Black Americans have not been the most impacted over time. By 2021, Native American communities had endured the worst of the pandemic in America and Hispanic Americans suffered higher rates of hospitalization and mortality. By summer 2021, Black Americans were still seeing nearly three times the number of hospitalizations and twice the number of deaths from COVID compared to white Americans, stemming from a nearly identical number of infections.

Likewise, as the economic course of 2020 became set and the disruption of businesses brought massive layoffs and soaring unemployment, Black Americans found themselves disproportionately placed at the forefront of the downturn. By the end of the year, unemployment for Black Americans had soared to 9.9 percent compared with 6 percent among white Americans. Concurrently, as the pandemic ravaged America's small business community, Black businesses were among those hit hardest. By April 2020, 41 percent of Black businesses, 440,000 individual companies, had closed their doors compared with 17 percent of white-owned businesses. And though help was eventually offered, it was typically uneven in distribution.

While the Payroll Protection Program had a number of well-publicized issues, few were as glaring as the racial disparities in the disbursement of funds and the amount of time it took for Black- and Hispanic-owned businesses to receive aid. Major banks demonstrably eschewed Black businesses, which were forced to turn to online lenders as their major sources of credit. More loans were given to businesses located in ZIP codes with majority white populations, while businesses in Black and Hispanic neighborhoods waited longer for the few loans that were awarded to them to arrive. At every crucial point of the crisis, it became clear that the situation was worse for America's communities of color. And the connecting element in many of these instances was home.

The impact of centuries of discriminatory real estate practices were felt in new ways in 2020 as Black households in crowded cities or high-occupancy rental properties found them to be clear obstacles to social distancing and other healthful measures. Connected issues of food and environmental injustice gained new attention as major factors in the prevalence of preexisting conditions within Black communities. And already established conversations on medical equity received a much-needed boost as questions were raised about the level of care afforded to Black Americans.

The wealth and wage gaps also took on new dimensions of importance as it became clear who in America could afford to maintain their household during the crisis, who had the ability to work from home, who had access to health care and protective equipment—and who, on the other hand, was deemed "essential." Meanwhile, the practices of banks charged with supporting struggling businesses revealed shadows of the ongoing practice of redlining as Black neighborhoods were targeted for avoidance, delays, and lower standards of service.

In a moment where the importance of home for all Americans was most apparent, Black Americans found themselves most at risk of losing theirs. While moratoriums on evictions and foreclosures offered temporary respite, a massive surge in both continues to loom, with little question as to which communities will be most affected.

In almost every instance, the events of 2020 did not create unfair or disadvantaged situations for Black people; they simply exacerbated inequalities that were already at work and that had come about, not by chance, but by deliberate and methodical disenfranchisement enacted on several levels in and around the process of buying homes. As a result, the loss of Black homes following any natural disaster or market collapse is a highly visible and predictable pattern, the repetition of which in 2020 demonstrated once again the ways in which American society acts to ensure that communities of color—particularly, though not solely, Black communities—will be the hardest hit by any calamity, and the slowest to recover.

OFF THE BEATEN PATH

Getaways, hideaways, and farmhouses—the homes that defy the stereotypes of "urban living" and reveal untapped layers of the African American experience.

Collectors of sculptures from around the globe, Jeanine Hays and Bryan Mason have worked to integrate sculptures both inside and outside of their home. On the outdoor dining table sits an Ife head that they discovered in a souk in Morocco.

TRECI AND AMIR SMITH: BUILDING A LEGACY

TRECI SMITH AND HER HUSBAND, AMIR, live in a Southern
California home that was never intended to be owned by Black people.
When it was first built, the original deed to the land was written with
a race covenant: a then–legally binding addendum stipulating that
the home and the land it's situated on could only be bought or sold by
someone white. That they've spent the last thirteen years frustrating
the racist intent of the original landowner is only one of the many things
that they enjoy about their home. Another is imagining that person's
face if they could see what they've done with it.

The Smith estate is vast, with area enough to encompass a
2,300-square-foot main house, an 1,100-square-foot guest house, and
an 800-square-foot studio office—with plenty of room to spare. Adding
atmosphere to the home's several structures is an expansive outdoor
area, including a full lounge space, a garden (complete with a chicken
coop), and a pool. "And there's still part of the yard that we haven't even
done anything with," Amir says with a laugh.

Though they grew up in Southern California, both Treci and Amir
originally hail from the Midwest. Their families arrived in the region in
the 1920s and 1930s, having left the South during the early days of the
Great Migration.

Treci comes from a traveling family. The youngest daughter of a

Right:
A boomerang coffee table
stands at the center of this
retro living room, where the
curved white sofa dominates.
It's the perfect space for
relaxing and listening
to Amir's jazz collection.

Above:
In the family room, a blue
velvet sofa adds a soft yet
modern touch.

Opposite:
The brick fireplace has been
painted black. The dark shade
allows the floral-upholstered
chairs and amber glass lamps
to truly shine in the family
room.

Navy master chief, her family followed her father's career to several stations before settling finally in San Diego. Yet her earliest memories are of a home in Indianapolis that they bought when she was seven.

"It was our first single-family home," she remembers. And while the experience remains foundational for her, it's one that she remembers more in essence than in detail. "I really only remember two things about that home," she explains. "One was helping my dad build a deck out back. The other was that my mom had drawn Charlie Brown figures on the walls in the bedroom I shared with my sister. That's it. It's funny, but I can't remember anything else."

What did stick with Treci was the feeling of the home. "There was just this sense of security, having all of us in that home together. I have three siblings. It was the four of us growing up together, playing cards, listening to music. We moved a lot but that was my first memory, feeling safe at home." It was a sensation that her mother carried to every home they had throughout her father's career and that ignited Treci's own interest in design.

"My mom taught me at an early age that different homes require

a different design, different style," she says, "which I think is how I inherited the design gene." It was a lesson that would be repeated as the family left Indianapolis to make stops in the Bay Area and Virginia Beach. Then came San Diego and high school, where she would meet Amir.

Originally from St. Louis, Amir arrived in California with his mother following his parents' separation. Prior to that, he lived in an apartment with his parents. His most vivid memories of home, however, are of the houses his grandparents owned, one of which his paternal grandmother still owns. "I remember the basement of that house was the music room. There were drums and a bar and, of course, a record player with a serious collection of jazz."

After moving to California, homeownership would remain a distant dream for Amir's mother, owing in part to rampant interest rates. "We lived in apartments and in low-income housing," he recalls. "Even though my mother was a working professional with a degree in accounting, we still couldn't afford to buy a place." The experience stayed with him, shaping what would become a longtime interest in real estate.

Though the couple met in high school, they didn't date initially. They exchanged numbers when they connected again years later, but both were in relationships. It wasn't until both courtships had run their course that they found themselves gravitating toward each other. "It just felt right," Treci says with a smile. "I knew that he would be my husband."

Like their relationship, the design of Treci and Amir's home is a seamless blend of their personal aesthetics that just feels right. Admittedly, it's not a hard combination to achieve. "Our styles are pretty similar at this point," Treci observes. "For one, we married so young that we kind of grew up together. It also helps that I like to design the interior while his aesthetic is more the outdoors." It's a dynamic that reminds Treci of her own parents, whose styles enjoyed a similar dichotomy.

The Smith family aesthetic is a blend of vintage and midcentury with a heavy nod toward the 1970s. Warm wood floors cover the whole of the interior, joined in the family's open-plan dining and family room by a wood-paneled ceiling and a brick feature wall painted in a deep black. Patterned chairs, long-necked vases, wicker baskets, and hanging plants all do their part in the room to complete the throwback feel. For both Treci and Amir, it's a style that draws directly from the homes they grew up in. "Home always felt very warm," Treci reminisces. "Lots of warm colors and furniture and texture that makes you feel like you want to just climb on the couch and nest." Even the wall decor carries a '70s vibe. The back wall of the dining room boasts a brass sunburst piece, populated by small birds. Beneath it sits the most important art piece in the house: a framed portrait of the couple on their wedding day.

Before they got married, Treci worked in finance and for an airline, while Amir took a job with a local utility company—a company he still works for today. Two years after the wedding, the couple marked the arrival of their first child, Zuri, who was followed by Zoe, Zamira, and finally Nicholas. For most of the time since the birth of their first child Treci has worked at home, caring for the children and crafting their environment.

Like the family room, the living room is built for comfort as much as for style. "With four kids, we can't have a home that doesn't function," Treci says, laughing. "It's one of the reasons I like midcentury so much. Everything's so comfortable." For Amir, the real focus of the room sits in the back: a vintage walnut record cabinet that holds a lot of memories. "My father had a room full of albums, a player, and a big pillow," he recalls. "Of course there was Coltrane in there and Miles Davis, Thelonious Monk, and Cole Porter. So in this room we kind of re-created that."

In owning a home, Amir had captured something that had eluded his parents for some time. He saw the potential in real estate to provide not only a home for his family, but also a future. It was the coming to fruition of an idea that had been planted in him when he was a teenager. "I was eighteen years old," he begins, "and I was going to this barber, Mr. Gentry, who was like a grandfather to me. He had his shop, and he would buy houses here and there. He had sixteen or twenty rental houses, and he would always tell me that real estate was the way to get my money working. And that really stuck in my head. I was just soaking it up."

"Even if it's a little condo or a little apartment or a little house, you can make it your own."

It started in the mid-nineties with Amir partnering with a coworker to purchase one house in Temecula, California. From there real estate became an ongoing part of their lives. Eventually, Amir and Treci began buying other properties in California and Indiana on their own. It was a process that opened new doors for Treci as well.

"When we got ready to sell the first house, Treci staged it. It sold quickly, and we did well," Amir says. "So that was like the 'aha' moment for all of us."

"I feel like it was something I always did," Treci reflects, "but now it had a title." It didn't take long for people to ask if "stager" could also mean "designer." "Suddenly I had friends and neighbors who would ask about what I could help them do in their homes." Her dream has turned into a new profession, complete with an office space she had built in the backyard.

Amir's office is a perfect gentleman's
lounge, with deep black walls and
a Chesterfield sofa. A piece by family
friend, Tomasha, of hip-hop artist
Rakim hangs over the desk.

A mix of vintage Indian kantha pillows
add color to the bedroom. The floral-
rich patterns are echoed in the brass
wall art above the bed.

Each child's room was designed to have its own personal aesthetic. In this room, a mauve daybed is enveloped in shades of purple.

Above:
Treci carves out a cozy seating area in the main bedroom with a mix of modern and vintage elements.

Opposite:
Treci, Amir, their daughters Zuri, Zoe, Zamira, and their son Nicholas sit by the pool in the backyard.

The business of home has been good to the Smiths, be it the home that they live in, the ones they've purchased, or the ones that Treci designs. The couple even transformed their detached garage into a guesthouse, which they run as a bed-and-breakfast.

It's also provided an ideal environment for their children to grow, learn, and find paths of their own. The group has pursued majors in anthropology, mechanical engineering, public health, and business, with Nicholas already looking to make his own entrée into the family business of buying and selling homes.

"He's picked up a lot from both of us," Treci says. "He likes design more than the girls, and he's already trying to find a place for them to invest in together." Seeing the story move into its next generation reinforces what Amir has always believed about the importance of owning a home.

"Anything's possible," he reflects. "Even if it's a little condo or a little apartment or a little house, you can make it your own. If you can get this, it can change the direction of your family."

CHRIS GLASS:
BEING SEEN

IN TERMS OF VISIBILITY, Chris Glass seems hard to miss. A trained and experienced performer, soft-spoken yet well-traveled, charming but believable, he doesn't struggle to command attention. In fact, he's the perfect choice for his role as Soho House's head of membership for Europe and Africa. Looking out the window of his two-bedroom flat in the city of Berlin, it's hard to believe that this longtime expat was once a young boy in Georgia who struggled with feelings of invisibility.

"I always knew that I would need to go far away because Atlanta didn't feel big enough for me," reflects Chris Glass. Now more than four thousand miles away from his native Georgia, the former actor and singer admits that living on another continent wasn't his first idea. Nevertheless, he exclaims, "I was fascinated by Europe. I was constantly traveling from city to city and country to country. After a year, I just couldn't imagine leaving."

But it was more than just the easy travel that attracted Chris to his new home. Like scores of African Americans before him, he found the experience of being in Europe to be very different from America. While exploring Europe, he found something that he'd been seeking for a very long time. "I felt seen," he says, smiling. "For the first time, as a man of color. Suddenly I wasn't defined by the color of my skin, being onstage, or my parents' expectations. Finally, I felt like I was carving my own path."

Right:
Chris's home features a
stunning collection of
objets d'art. Crucifixes,
phallic candles, and African
sculpture play among each
other on his floor-to-ceiling
shelves.

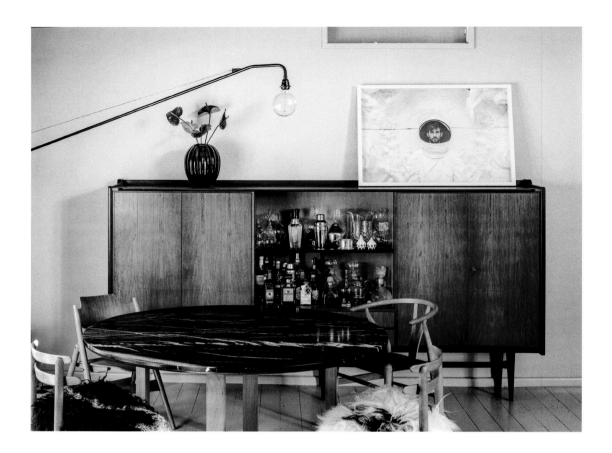

Above:
Chris is a collector of
midcentury modern furnishings.
In the dining room, a
midcentury cabinet perfectly
complements the Hans Wegner
Wishbone Chairs.

As a child, Chris was naturally sensitive to how he fit into the scheme of things. His ability to do so seamlessly contributed to his own sense of anonymity. "I behaved well," he reflects, "being the person that I was taught to be and staying within the lines." But when a teacher noticed a creative energy in need of expression, it was brought to his parents' attention. His mother, a chemist for the Environmental Protection Agency, and his father, who'd inherited his profession as a florist from his own father, were intrigued. "In their confusion and fascination," he explains, "my parents put me in acting classes."

The theater appeared to be Chris's way out of his shell. Training in singing, acting, and dance revealed a natural talent for music. "I was more of a singer than an actor," he remembers, "and more of an actor than a dancer." It all quickly coalesced into a new identity. "It was sort of understood very early on that Chris was going to be a performer," he says.

For a time, Chris admits that theater was his escape. But eventually he found that getting attention and being seen weren't the same thing. "Even though I was escaping into these characters, I felt very defined by

The bedroom features some beautiful artisan items, including a hand-embroidered suzani blanket and handmade ceramic lamps.

my environment," he remembers. Ironically, Chris found that the more attention he received, the easier it was to hide and the more impossible it became to define himself. "So it was this very strange combination," he reflects. "Performing wasn't something my parents encouraged, but it was how everyone knew me. It didn't make me feel alive, but I would have felt dead without it." Yet despite his inner conflicts, theater continued to be his way forward. After graduating from a performing arts high school, Chris attended the Boston Conservatory. He would eventually leave Boston for New York, "with seventy-five dollars in my pocket, a book of songs I could sing, and stacks of CDs packed into little books because that was what you did back then."

It was the quintessential life of a creative living in New York: Chris bounced between auditions and a series of unsatisfying jobs until he came to the attention of the owners of a small cosmetics start-up who offered him a position, managing their shop in Munich. It was an amazing opportunity, but there's nothing more challenging than convincing a New Yorker to leave New York City, so it took Chris's new employers more than a year and a half to convince him to relocate. When they succeeded, it was the start of his new life as an expat. Eight years later, he was on the move again, this time from Munich to Berlin. "I really needed a place that was more stimulating and dynamic," he remarks.

Leaving for Berlin led to Chris working for Soho House and starting the next part of his journey. Unbeknownst to him, it would also signal the beginning of his life in design. As travel broadened his horizons, Chris discovered a new joy of home— creating the environment that he wanted to live in. "It was one of the first times that I was able to make choices for myself that other people had to accept," he recalls.

> ## "I try to create spaces that are harmonious. And within that harmony there are layers of stories to tell."

His Berlin home has become his canvas for self-expression. "In my childhood home there were colors and patterns that, at the time, I found extremely sophisticated and unusual," Chris recalls. As a result, his own home uses color in subtle yet impactful ways. Bright colors don't leap from the walls, yet the shades Chris chooses never fail to make an impression, providing context for everything that the room is intended to be. In his bedroom, a unique shade of mauve is a direct reference to his mother's tastes and the impression they made on him. "I remember her talking about the color *mauve*," he reminisces. "Of course, as a ten-year-old I had no idea what she was talking about. But it sounded like the coolest thing."

In his bedroom, the color strikes the perfect note of serenity with

Opposite:
A vintage retro TOGO sofa from
Ligne Roset rests in Chris's
home office.

none of the sterility implied by more expected neutral colors. Paired with earth tones, global patterns, and the room's overall minimalist aesthetic, it conveys a sense of its well-traveled occupant while also giving him a sense of home. "As a kid it felt like my bedroom was hidden away from the world. There was a window I could peek out, and I could see the world the way I wanted to see it. That's how I feel about my bedroom now."

Other more tangible mementos have made the long trip from Atlanta to Germany: "There's artwork of two little boys that hung in my bedroom when I was young. I went home and found it a few years ago and brought it back. It reminds me of my relationship with my brother and that bedroom and now I have it in my home." Another cherished memory sits on his coffee table, made all the more precious because it represents a memory that Chris himself doesn't have.

"My mother gave me a toy gun," he says with a laugh. "I'm not a fan of guns, but I wanted this one. My grandfather carved it out of wood for me when I was a newborn, but he died before I ever knew him." His mother had kept the toy for years, but lost track of it. When it resurfaced, she offered it to Chris. "I didn't know if I was going to be able to get it into Germany," he explains, "because I didn't know what they'd think about it at the airport."

The living room is a scene that expands from eclectic to comprehensive, verging on all-inclusive. In a visual frame created by a rug cleverly deployed to mimic the texture and color of the room's concrete walls with near perfection, the erstwhile performer has combined so many elements that nearly every one has a complementary opposite somewhere else in the room: For every plant there's a metallic. For every midcentury piece, a modern sculpture. Every graphic encouraging readers to BE AMAZING is followed by another admonishing them to SAVE YOUR ASS, or simply FUCK. And for every crucifix or Buddha, there's a skull or a candle shaped like a giant phallus.

"I have a lot of phalluses in my home," he ponders. "I don't know why. I also have a lot of religious iconography and a couple of other things." The collection of crosses continues into his hallway where a drastic reversal in color provides an equally suitable backdrop for his collections. "I try to create spaces that are harmonious. And within that harmony there are layers of stories to tell."

Of all the tools a designer has to tell a story or convey an idea, art is by far the most direct. The statements that cover the walls in Chris's home range from the very direct to the most oblique. His collection includes photo portraits of himself alongside framed posters of gallery exhibits and works by Ernie Barnes, the African American pro

Above:
The hallway is a gallery unto
itself, painted in a deep, dark
green and featuring an array
of black-and-white art. A neon
cross adds the final pop
of color.

Opposite:
The kitchen shelving is
a home to an artful display
of knickknacks that Chris
has collected over time.

football player–turned–artist whose paintings appeared in the series
Good Times.

Nestled in among the art and the icons are other treasures,
reminders of places like Turkey and Barcelona, where he's lived for
as much as a year. They sit with mementos of a hundred different
excursions to all the parts of the globe that he's seen since arriving in
Germany. "It's very much a collection of places where I've spent time,"
he confides. "But it wasn't about collecting, just interesting and special
things that I've discovered along the way."

In design, Chris found the last piece of a puzzle that he had been
assembling for a very long time. "Design has been an integral part of
me seeing myself because it was the first expression of myself that I
felt like I owned for myself. No one taught me to do it. I wasn't doing it
for someone else. It's something that I cultivated and developed on my
own. It was the first time in my life that I felt like I could stand in the
fullness of a thing, and allow myself to claim it. And that gave me the
self-confidence to claim who I am."

CAMILLE AND JOE SIMMONS: FINDING A FAIRY TALE

CAMILLE AND JOE SIMMONS have history. The pair of Long Beach, California, natives met just after graduating from high school together. But there's more. It's a story that starts with two families moving west during the Great Migration, when some six million African Americans migrated from the American South. While many went north to find new promise, Camille and Joe's families headed for California.

Camille's family arrived in Los Angeles in the early days of the migration. "My mom's family actually had been in California for a little bit," she begins. "My great-grandfather was from Mississippi and my great-grandmother was from Baton Rouge, Louisiana." By the early 1900s both of her great-grandparents had made their way out to Carmel, where they met at a church revival. "They got married, moved to LA, and my grandfather was born in Los Angeles in 1922."

Her father's family was only a few decades behind. Born in Mobile, Alabama, Camille's father migrated to California with his family in the 1940s when he was only two. Following other family members to Northern California, the entire family eventually made their way to Los Angeles.

"They won't say Watts," she says with a laugh. "They only say it was Watts-adjacent. But that was pretty much the only place where Black families could buy homes because of the way LA was sectioned off.

Right:
Camille and Joe made the space
their own, adding Rifle Paper
Company's Fable wallpaper
to the living room wall and
a painting of the couple
that was made for them as
a wedding present.

Above:
The home office has a
collection of some of the
couple's favorite retro
items, from milk glass
accessories to a Crosley
record player.

Opposite:
Camille was able to get
her grandparents' piano
transported from Los Angeles
to their home in the San
Bernardino mountains.
It's a family heirloom with
a lot meaning.

There were only certain suburbs, and Watts was the big one before World War II. Even Compton was still very white."

Camille and Joe have tried piecing together their family narratives, but it's been hard. When older generations have escaped lives of pain and violence, they're often eager to forget and reluctant to share. "People don't talk about things," Camille confirms. "We did a road trip to Texas once, where my mom's mother is from. I tried to do some digging on family history, but everybody's so hush-hush." Joe's experience has been the same. "I only know three things about my great-grandmother on my mom's father's side," he offers. "She was born in Tennessee, she met Martin Luther King, and she moved to California after leaving her husband."

The couple is trying to create something different for their son, Milo, helping him build roots in his own home, a cottage located in the San Bernadino Mountains. For Camille, who was just eight when her mother bought her first house, this moment is particularly meaningful. It was in her first house growing up that she became enamored with design. "I just saw the decorating craziness explode. Suddenly I was

Right:
Milo's bedroom is a dreamy
space for him to grow and
play in. A pair of vintage
beds completes the fairy-tale
cottage feel of the space.

getting dragged to showrooms and stores. I just remember furniture coming in and swatches being everywhere," she says with a smile. And she now sees Milo having a similar experience as his parents design their first home.

The process also has her reflecting on her grandmother, whom she lived just miles away from as a girl, and who showed her how to make a house a home. "When I was a little girl, she was always sewing blankets or curtains," she says of her grandmother. "I was developing an eye for what I liked and I see the roots of my decor style in hers—very bright, there's grays and whites but lots of pops of color." Camille credits her grandmother as well for showing her the importance of representing culture in decor. "She was really big on that. Her home had a lot of Egyptian-based art, images of Nefertiti, and different artworks but very clean lines—like she was trying to infuse African details into a very traditional home."

In the cottage, Camille has her grandmother's piano on display in the living room as a way of keeping her close. The house has a fairy-tale feel to it, with beautiful archways, stained glass, and stunning murals. It's a perfect place for a child to grow up and dream in. From the living room's bright pops of pink to Milo's bedroom, which is a whimsical woodland retreat, each room has been lovingly designed with comfort in mind. And Camille and Joe have made it all happen with their own two hands.

> ## "There's so much bias and no understanding of how different the world is for Black people. We felt like we just couldn't compete."

"Growing up, we had a two-story, three-bedroom townhouse that my parents and I shared with my aunt at first," Joe remembers. "We had an automotive fabricator next door. He would have people bring over their race cars and he would do a lot of metalwork. So I learned a lot about working with metal going over there." For Joe, a mechanical engineer who is starting a new career path in craft brewing, the return to nature and renovating the new home means finding new ways to work with his hands. "We built all of the exterior handrails around the house using cut branches and fallen branches from the cedar and pine trees out front and dried wood from around the house. I stripped off the bark, anchored it into the ground and reinforced it with rocks. And it looks really good," he remarks.

While they have loved working on their new house, the journey to owning their first home was not a fairy tale. The couple faced many of the hardships that Black homebuyers commonly experience. "When we first started looking, our intention was to rent an apartment for a year or two while we looked for a house in Long Beach," Joe says. It was

Camille and Joe commissioned a
mural for the bedroom wall. And
carved shelving in a Moroccan
motif creates space for Milo's
favorite toys and books.

during that time that Camille's popular interior design blog, *Planning Pretty*, took the form of a brick-and-mortar shop located just around the corner from the couple's two-bedroom walk-up apartment. It was in the same area they were hoping to buy in.

Despite a favorable market and sufficient savings, the couple ran into an all-too-familiar set of problems for African American homebuyers. "We dealt with a lot of racism," Camille relates, "which we didn't expect because, you know, it's Long Beach. We grew up here. We already live here. But the realtors, especially the selling agents, were very biased." With a particular type of home in mind they quickly found that the gates of homeownership in their area were tightly guarded— and they were being blocked at every path.

"We tried everything," Joe remembers. "Every time we sent out a new offer letter, we'd include photos of us and Milo and our pets. We were a nice couple, our finances were good, Camille had a small business in the area, we could bid pretty high, and we made strong offers. And we would be rejected over and over again. That was three years. There's so much bias," Joe marvels, "and no understanding of how different the world is for Black people. We felt like we just couldn't compete."

The journey to finding a home became even more urgent when their son was diagnosed with a serious health issue. "Milo was diagnosed with leukemia at three months," Joe says, "and it just totally blew us away." For a time their house hunt ground to a halt as they searched for treatment options for their son.

Milo is now in remission, following a two-month stay at a children's hospital at the height of the 2020 pandemic, but the family's return home coincided with the outbreak of California's wildfire season. "There was so much going on when we came back," Joe remembers. "We just kept thinking about how it would impact him. Just as they were starting to reexamine their ambition to own a home in Long Beach, Camille and Joe found their mountain retreat.

"That market was competitive as well," Camille relates, "but not as bad. The people up there were a little bit more accepting. It was still a long process," she says, "but the communication was easier." Most important, it was the right decision for Milo. "The irony of moving to a forest is that this one is actually away from the fires so the air quality is five times better up here," Joe says. "And when we first visited, Milo loved it. So it just kind of felt like the natural place to be."

As California natives, with so many of their own childhood memories revolving around time spent in nature, Camille and Joe were excited to give Milo the same opportunities. "We thought, 'Alright, let's give him this chance.' You don't see very many Black boys this far out in nature on the West Coast. So we wanted to give him that opportunity.

Above:
In the dining room, the home's floral theme continues with a rug that looks like a bed of green ivy.

Opposite:
In the home office, pattern on pattern play brings the outdoors in, with floral wallpaper, drapery, and upholstery on the side chair.

And he's loving it. He's small, but he drags us everywhere. We can just open the door, and he's ready to go." Camille is currently teaching him to tend the garden around the house.

Life is made up of journeys. Before they were even born, Camille and Joe's families took the journey west, hoping to find something better for their children. Today, the couple has taken on their own journey, searching for a safe place that their son can call home. "I think everything that we've tried to do, through our whole relationship, has been about making sure that we are comfortable with what we're choosing," says Joe. "It may not always look like what anyone expects. But all we can do is make sure that we're intentional about whatever we're choosing—the actions we take, the things put in our house, or what we personally do so that when we look back, we can say that it was what we wanted."

MEMORIES OF HOME

Above:
Milo enjoying his fairy-tale-inspired bedroom.

Opposite:
A tepee tent in the corner is a favorite play area for Milo. On the bookshelf are some special family heirlooms, including a painting of Milo by his grandfather and a hand-carved wooden biplane that honors the family's lineage in aerospace.

JOE: Both of our families have a long history in aerospace. My step-grandfather was a computer contractor for aerospace companies and my dad's father was in the Air Force and later worked for an aerospace company.

CAMILLE: My grandfather was a pilot. He was in Burma during World War II, and when he came back to the US, he learned to fly. There was a Black pilots club at the Compton airport, and he and his brother had a plane there. He also worked in aerospace around parts and materials, and was the president of his union. My grandparents had a beautifully decorated house, they had a swimming pool, and they had a plane. It was a Black middle-class family home that we don't often think of as being possible in the '40s and '50s. So whenever Milo sees a plane, we want him to know that it's a part of his family's history.

—**Camille and Joe Simmons**

JEANINE HAYS AND BRYAN MASON: THE MEANING OF HOME

WE BOTH COME FROM FAMILIES in which homeownership is considered very important. Our parents, grandparents, and even great-grandparents all had homes of their own. We grew up in these spaces, were shaped by the things we learned in them, and became inspired by their design. Yet for much of our lives, homeownership wasn't a goal we pursued as we moved between Philadelphia, Washington, DC, San Francisco, and Brooklyn. But life's unexpected turns eventually brought us to the Hudson Valley and our beloved AphroFarmhouse.

Our story of home began the day we met. In our senior year of high school we were leaving from Philadelphia International Airport for a weeklong tour of Florida A&M. We didn't know each other or attend the same school. But we spoke in the airport, and again on the plane—and we've been together ever since. Instead of Florida A&M, we spent four years in a long-distance relationship between Drexel Unversity in Philadelphia and Spelman College in Atlanta. After Jeanine graduated, we lived together for the first time in an apartment near Drexel's West Philadelphia campus.

Looking at our first apartment, there was little to suggest that our futures lay in interior design. It was Bryan's bachelor pad, complete with hand-me-down furniture and an old television set. It had all the design savvy of an overworked IT major with no knowledge and less

Right:
The living room blends rustic
elements like the burl wood
table with artisan pieces,
including the handloomed
Moroccan rug. An oversized
bubble chandelier adds a sense
of sophistication to the space.

Above:
The living room is filled with feminine energy in the form of art and sculpture. "Sisters" by artist Mafalda Vasconcelos and the Bootyful Black Bum Vase from Latzio represent the beauty of the Black female form.

Opposite:
The home features works by artists from around the globe, including Baltimore sculptor Murjoni Merriweather and artisans from Nigeria.

interest in what made a room work. But it was perfect in its way: a generous living room with a galley kitchen that fed through French doors into a cozy bedroom. It was where we learned that we love to cook together, that we love listening to jazz on Sundays, and that a whole day spent together doing anything is the best thing that we can ever do with our time.

After Bryan graduated from Drexel, we lived together in Washington, DC, where Jeanine attended American University's Washington College of Law. There, we lived in a charismatic two-bedroom apartment in DC's Eastern Market neighborhood with Jeanine's sister, Angela, while she attended Howard University.

DC was where we took our first steps toward design. Jeanine had been fascinated with it since she decorated her first room as a child—an all-pink affair in honor of Strawberry Shortcake. Choosing between a law degree and interior design school had been a close decision. But once she was immersed in the law, design became her escape. Time spent in bookstores was a constant hunt for shelter magazines and design books. And when Angela moved into her own apartment, the

Right:
The library is a play on the couple's favorite color: blue. Furnishings in the shade were brought in to layer color into the room. Blue-and-white chairs featuring AphroChic's Batik fabric break up the color block.

In the dining room, works from two of
the couple's favorite artists represent
the warrior spirit of Black women: "The
Samurai Princess" by Tim Okamura and
"The Honesty of Bronze" by Fares Micue.

second bedroom became a yoga studio painted in a trendy pink and brown color palette. It was also where Jeanine first dreamed of writing a book on interior design, something to express design as she was coming to see it.

The city was a constant source of inspiration. Visits to the Smithsonian were a weekly habit. Any given day could find us exploring exhibits at the National Museum of African Art; taking in the works at the National Museum of Asian Art; or walking through the Sculpture Garden at the Hirshhorn Museum. DC was where we saw the works of Jacob Lawrence and Frida Kahlo up close for the first time. It was also the place where we found our voices as activists, protesting in front of the Supreme Court and participating in marches and rallies for equity and justice.

Just out of law school, Jeanine was offered a job with an anti-domestic violence nonprofit organization in San Francisco. As it happened, Bryan had been considering a grad school in the Bay area as well. Though we loved DC, the decision and the move both happened quickly—at the start of the week we lived in DC, by the end we were Californians.

> "We spoke in the airport, and again on the plane—and we've been together ever since."

San Francisco is where AphroChic was born. But it took time. During our first years there, Jeanine was engaging her political mind, working on policy initiatives that mattered deeply to her. Meanwhile, Bryan was on the path to becoming an academic. A master's degree in theology led to the University of California at Berkeley and a second master's in African Diaspora studies.

On the weekends, we would walk the city's hills, discovering hidden gems, like Diego Rivera murals in a school courtyard or Noguchi's work in an antiques shop. The city was at once a trove of interesting midcentury design and a burgeoning hub of business and technology. We had arrived in the lull between the fall of the dot-coms and the rise of Silicon Valley. Just about everyone seemed to be working for a start-up or creating one themselves. It was a place that supported the idea of stepping out on your own, and it inspired us to do just that.

The *AphroChic* blog debuted in the spring of 2007, an effort to address the lack of representation for people of color in the design field. Two years later we started making products after realizing how few home décor accessories were created for or marketed to people of the African Diaspora. Taking advantage of the city's tech focus, we printed our pillows on one of the first dye sublimation machines in the country.

San Francisco was also the beginning of our design aesthetic. We

Opposite:
The home's main bedroom
features an array of delicate
florals, from embroidered
suzani pillows to a handloomed
Persian rug featuring a
floral print.

had a beautiful apartment, at the top of the Embarcadero, just a block away from the pier and the bay. It was a clean, modern, one-bedroom California white box with more space than anything we were used to. For two weeks after we arrived we lived in the dining room because we were scared to move into the rest of the apartment. But when we did, Jeanine began to fill the space with beautiful things she discovered in the city: juju hats, vintage accessories, and a handmade dining table. A walk-in coat closet became a wallpapered office with modern light fixtures. It was light-years ahead of what she'd done in DC, but still only the start of where we were going.

After six years in San Francisco we returned home to Philadelphia, taking our first steps as full-time entrepreneurs. Virtually nothing had changed about Philly in the years since we'd been gone, but everything had changed about the way we saw the city and how we felt about it. We moved into the historic neighborhood of Old City and realized how much of Philadelphia's rich history is Black history. Our walk-up apartment—in a building which had originally been America's second bank—was just a short distance from the excavated slave quarters of George Washington's Philadelphia home. Equally close was the waterfront where enslaved Africans once disembarked from ships and Mother Bethel church, founded by Richard Allen, which still stands on the country's oldest parcel of land continuously owned by African Americans.

Living in the city where W.E.B. DuBois wrote *The Philadelphia Negro*, Francis Johnson became America's first international music star, and Richard Allen's church hosted the first Black "protest" meeting gave us a deeper perspective on the importance of our work as Black designers. We recognized history as an essential component of culture, just as culture was inextricably tied to design, bringing new dimensions to our idea of "narrative" in design.

After four years in Philadelphia, we were in need of growth and new creative challenges. Brooklyn was our only choice. We'd fallen in love with the borough while living in San Francisco, through frequent visits when Jeanine's sister was living there. And we knew it was the next place we wanted to call home.

We lived in a beautiful part of Crown Heights, on the third floor of a 200-year-old brownstone. Our apartment was a miraculous find. Twelve hundred square feet, divided between a huge living room, a generous bedroom, and a stand-alone kitchen, all connected by long hallways. Just like in San Francisco, we spent our first weeks in just one room without enough furniture or nerve to occupy the whole space.

By the time it was done, the design of our Brooklyn home was the perfect representation of where we were as AphroChic at the time:

modern, soulful, and culturally representative. We had an entire hallway wallpapered with one of our most popular patterns, Sisters, and a portrait of Melba Moore hung over the bed in our jet-black bedroom.

Again we were blessed with a perfect location. The Brooklyn Museum and Prospect Park were only a short, scenic walk away. We enjoyed design events and art gallery openings, rooftop parties and concerts at the parks—classical in Central, hip-hop and R&B in Prospect and jazz in Fort Greene. Best of all, we had a seemingly limitless community of Black creatives to enjoy. People who understood what we were doing and why. We knew we would call Brooklyn home forever, but then 2020 came and changed everything.

Bryan's illness started early in 2020, just as the whispers about a quickly spreading disease were beginning to grow. It took him months to recover, and, as he did, Jeanine began to experience an array of strange allergic reactions. Antibody tests would eventually reveal that we both had suffered from COVID-19, and Jeanine had developed what would eventually be called "long haul" Covid.

As 2020 wore on, it became clear that the city was no longer a tenable situation for us. Twelve hundred square feet isn't much to live in when you can't access the rest of the city, even less when you're struggling with respiratory issues caused by a virus. As we started to look at the possibility of life outside of Brooklyn, suddenly a house made much more sense. We were in need of a space where we could heal and we made the decision to move upstate.

Because of the way that we came into this house and the health difficulties that we faced, designing this home was about more than creating a look—it was a celebration of recovery, from painting the rooms together to placing the last book on the shelf. We've always said that design tells a story. After so much time together and so much story between us, this house had a lot that it needed to say.

The west side of the Hudson Valley, where we live, is technically "mid-state." But for those like us whose concept of New York revolves mainly around the city, two hours from Brooklyn is worlds away. Missing the city, we sought to design a home that felt like Brooklyn, but with a country twist. Inside our 1930s farmhouse, safety, control, visibility, celebration, and memory, which we see as the essential elements of African American design, are woven into every room.

We started with color as a way to evoke a feeling of safety and serenity in every room in this house. In the living room, creamy, off-white walls bring an immediate feeling of tranquility. Paired with matching drapery, soft yet meaningful bursts of pink in the sofas, and the earth tones of the coffee tables, the colors combine for an air of total relaxation. A whimsical bubble chandelier was the perfect finishing touch to create a room so warm and comforting that as soon as it was complete, Jeanine took to calling it the "womb room." Distinctly feminist touches, such as paintings by Mozambican artist Mafalada Vasconcelos, inject color and meaning into the space. The feminine forms in the work complement the collection of African female sculptures Jeanine has been curating since living in DC. The female energy continues in the Moroccan rugs, handmade by women and imbued with artistry, history, and culture.

Complementing the living room, the library is a celebration of the masculine, and a wish fulfilled for Bryan—a place for our book collection to live and grow. Divided into a lounge area and a large reference table, the space is separated by built-in shelves teeming with books, art, and statuary. While the enveloping, deep blue walls provide their own feeling of security, this space speaks equally to themes of visibility and control.

Every book on the shelf is either by a Black author or about Black people. Academic studies and works of fiction or poetry sit beside design books, art compendiums, and graphic novels. The Black Panther makes more than one appearance. And some of our favorite books, specially displayed, stand in on the shelves as works of art. And while Shakespeare, Freire, Alcott, and other non-Black authors still make treasured contributions to our collection as a whole, our library is dedicated to representing and celebrating the work and history of Diaspora authors.

The reference table is flanked by stunning pieces from two of our favorite artists. Tim Okamura's "Samurai Princess" is one of many ancestral guardians watching over the house. She resides among a collection of Punu masks from Gabon, which represents the spirits of our ancestors. And an ethereal piece by photographer Fares Micue, of the Canary Islands, takes us into a beautiful secret garden.

On the second floor, we created a space completely dedicated to wellness. Energetic, terra cotta–colored walls, inspired by our time in Marrakech's Medina quarter, created the perfect atmosphere for boxing, yoga, and meditation. The walls in this room literally transform, transitioning easily into a guest bed when friends and family visit.

The main bedroom is a minimalist oasis. Like the living room, it uses a soft, putty wall color to create the feeling of a sanctuary—a place apart from the rest of the world. With little additional furniture allowed into the space, the room is dominated by the king-sized bed, crafted of American hardwood, yet still makes room for a cozy little reading nook.

> "We recognized history as an essential component of culture, just as culture was inextricably tied to design."

Above:
Jeanine and Bryan wanted
to bring the indoors out,
designing comfortable living
areas around the exterior
of their home. Their outdoor
living room is completed
with a stunning sculpture by
New York artist Jessica
Jean-Baptiste.

Memories are present in every room, reminders of everywhere we've lived and how much we've grown together. The African statues in the main bedroom were vintage finds in Washington, DC's Eastern Market. A small candy dish in the living room is a reminder of our time in San Francisco. And a small bust with amazing afro puffs was a custom-made piece for our apartment in Brooklyn.

The most meaningful pieces in our home are the heirlooms. In the kitchen, a secretary that once belonged to Bryan's great-grandmother was passed down to his grandmother and mother before finding new life in our kitchen in Brooklyn. Near it hangs a photo of one of Jeanine's cousins that she received from her father. Taken in the sixties, she cites it often as one of the inspirations for AphroChic.

Our farmhouse is filled, not just with the objects or stories, but with expressions of how we feel about each other, our families, and our culture. And though the road that brought us here was long, ultimately our story of home is very simple: One day at an airport two people spoke for the first time and realized that they were home. And they've been home ever since.

MEMORIES OF HOME

Above:
The couple worked with Italian firm Resource Furniture to custom design shelving that could hold their collection of Black literary works and art and design books from across the African Diaspora.

Opposite:
This home's expansive library is a dream come true. In it, books are treated as art. Favorite covers are on display, mixed with framed works from the couple's collection and a Punu mask from Gabon.

MY MOTHER'S FAMILY came up to Philadelphia from Virginia and South Carolina. My great-grandfather was a Pullman porter who moved north with his wife and children. My father's family came from South Carolina and Maryland. Both sides arrived in the early 1920s.

In Philly, it seems like family always lives "just around the corner." Our house was only a ten-minute drive from my grandmother's home. In the same time we could reach my mother's aunts, her cousins, my father's mother, father, brother, and more.

Looking back, that proximity was one of the best things about growing up. I was a shy kid, and didn't always have much to say, even to my family. But in those houses and all the time we spent picking things up or dropping them off, gathering for holidays, visiting or just stopping by, I felt how much love there was and is in my family. And I learned what it feels like to be home.

—Bryan Mason

MEMORIES OF HOME

Above:
In the living room sits another piece by artist Mafalda Vasconcelos entitled "Amma."

Opposite:
In the guest bedroom the bed features textiles from some of the couple's favorite brands: a set of pillows from South African brand Shine-Shine, and an AphroChic Sisters bolster. "Femme Sucree" from BetterShared artist Neals Niat adds a romantic note to the space.

MY MOTHER'S SIDE of the family came from Virginia. On that side they were traditionally teachers, as far back as the 1800s. My great-grandmother had a home in West Philadelphia, which is where most of my mom's side is from. She was a domestic worker, cleaning for white families, and my great-grandfather was a janitor who worked cleaning the hallways at Merck.

They had three daughters and sent all three to Cheney University—two became teachers. Their middle sister became a nurse. My great-grandmother had a lot of grandchildren and great-grandchildren. Growing up, we were always told that Great-grandma had to do domestic work, but she worked really hard so that we could always attain more, and homeownership and education were very important to her. So anytime someone got a new house, she just loved that because she had basically given us the foundation for all of that.

—Jeanine Hays

The Journey Home:
BRIDGING THE GAP— WEALTH, INHERITANCE & REPARATIONS

The story of the African American journey to home has been fraught with obstacles and hindrances, some circumstantial but most intentional—a struggle that began before America was a country and one that still continues today. Within our specific history, African Americans have had every American experience. We were both enslaved and free before the Civil War. We were also plantation owners, craftsmen, chefs, preachers, politicians, and soldiers. After the Civil War we were refugees. During the Great Migration we were essentially immigrants, our lives in new places often beginning with a single brave or fortunate traveler who worked and saved to bring other family members to a new home—with the same living conditions and job prospects as American immigrants in other times.

Since then we've been everything else and, in the span of a few centuries, we have created a culture that, like this nation, has impacted and shaped the world in various and inescapable ways. And in the shadow of that creation, the opposition and oppression laid against it also took shape.

From the beginning, the intended purpose of Black people's presence in America has been to provide for others the comforts and benefits that were perpetually denied to us. As time passed and things changed, that core perspective has remained, played out in numerous ways in nearly every aspect of American life. That the Black family home is a missing character in American history is part of the work this country has been doing since 1619 to send a very clear and direct message: that African Americans, and all Black people, are not at home in America.

But this is our home, and against all the headwinds of legal oppression, social violence, and economic marginalization, Black people have and will continue to make ourselves at home in the country that many of our ancestors helped to build and in which we all have a

An antique Kingsbury piano is on display
in the lounge. A piece from the Golden
Age of the Piano, it takes on new life as
a work of art in Jason Reynolds's salon.

interest. And in our continuing story
s value for all Americans.

our brief review of history shows, the
ity in homeownership rates between
ca's white and Black communities is
cidental, nor is it the result of choices
by individual Black households. Rather
e intended result of systemic practices
ing Black Americans from homebuying
tunities and resources. And though they
ely discussed, the purpose of these
rs is clear.

meownership is both a vital component
vidual wealth and a major building block
nerational wealth in America. As of 2019,
edian wealth of homeowners was found
orty times that of renters, with ownership
es widely cited as the major part of the
nce. And in terms of generational wealth

inheritances—which often include homes
have accounted for as much as 50 percent
the accumulation of household wealth in t
US throughout its history. Restricting acce
to homeownership therefore chokes off an
important potential source of growth to th
Black community, in turn limiting opportu
for education, business ownership, and
financial security.

Contrary to its bootstrapping self-imag
America has never lacked for homebuying
wealth-building programs. The emergenc
the American middle class is easily tracea
to a number of successful initiatives, from
GI Bill and the Federal Housing Administr
to the Homestead Act of 1862. That act gra
some 270 million acres of land to nearly
3 million people until 1986. And while a fev
African Americans were able to benefit fro

this program, racist practices in its enactment ensured that virtually all of the land allotted went to white owners. Yet to date, African Americans have never received such open entitlements and efforts to exclude Black Americans from those programs which do exist have yet to be meaningfully checked.

As a result, African Americans have perpetually experienced far lower homeownership rates than white Americans and consistently lower rates than any other racial group. Between 1870 and 2007, there has been at least a 20 percent gap in homeownership rates between the two communities, shrinking to 19 percent only once, in 1980. After the Great Recession, the rate of Black homeownership hovered around 41 percent, while the rate for white Americans soared to 72 percent. Yet despite generations of systematic discrimination, lack of individual effort and achievement by Black Americans are still thought of as the main causes for the discrepancy—which is why the Black family home remains a missing piece of our national story.

The historical absence of the Black family home operates as part of a series of overlapping oppressions woven into the fabric of American society. The cumulative effect of these is that oppression itself becomes hard to distinguish. Even when its impact is keenly felt, each layer lends a kind of plausible deniability to the others.

It's easy, for example, to dismiss the impact of discriminatory real estate and banking practices. Bankers and realtors merely have to point to the generally lower wages of Black Americans as reasons to deny loans or rationalize their absence from certain neighborhoods. The widely documented fact that employees of color are frequently paid substantially less than white employees for the same work is simply never mentioned. When Black communities are unable to endure an economic downturn, the suffering is explained as an unfortunate by-product of market forces, rather than the predictable outcome of specific practices in hiring, lending, housing, and more.

All of this serves to create a sense of happenstance around racial wealth disparities in America. While race is clearly a lens though which we view collective economic outcomes, racism has never factored into our solutions— until now. As calls for reparations come from those in high office and even the United Nations, it's being made clear that racist policies have been put in place to hinder Black people's advancement and that there must be redress. Yet while that battle continues, the Black family home continues to be what it has always been: a place of peace and abundant joy against the chaotic background of everything being done to make that place unreachable—a window on the still-surreal experience of Black American life.

The Black family home is more than a place. It's the feeling of being together with the people who love you and know you best. It's the pain of knowing all that the world has arrayed against you for nothing more than the color of your skin and the warm reassurance that you can face it all and win because it's been faced before. It's an accomplishment, an achievement, and the responsibility of ensuring that yours is not the only one. It's the fun of finding other homes, in other people from different parts of the world, tracing different histories, speaking different languages, and feeling the same because you are the same, just as much as you are unique. It's all of those things and none of them because sometimes it's where you go to sleep. It's just home.

Opposite:
This book-laden office in Jason Reynolds's home is filled to the brim with mementos, favorite art pieces, and works from the authors who inspire him to continue his work.

SELECTED BIBLIOGRAPHY

Bhutta, Neil, Andrew C. Chang, Lisa J. Dettling, Joanne W. Hsu, and Julia Hewitt. "Disparities in Wealth by Race and Ethnicity in the 2019 Survey of Consumer Finances." Board of Governors of the Federal Reserve System. Last modified September 28, 2020, https:// www.federalreserve.gov/econres/ notes/feds-notes/disparities-in-wealth-by-race-and- ethnicity-in-the-2019-survey-of-consumer-finances-20200928.htm.

Blackmon, Douglass A. *Slavery by Another Name: The Re-Enslavement of Black Americans from the Civil War to World War II.* New York: Anchor, 2008.

Blakemore, Erin. "How the GI Bill's Promise Was Denied to a Million Black WWII Veterans." History.com. Last updated April 20, 2021, https://www. history.com/news/gi-bill-black-wwii-veterans-benefits.

Brooks, Rodney A., "More than half of Black-owned businesses may not survive COVID-19." National Geographic. Last modified July 17, 2020, https:// api. nationalgeographic.com/distribution/public/amp/ history/article/black-owned-businesses-may-not-survive-covid-19.

Centers for Disease Control and Prevention. "Risk for COVID-19 Infection, Hospitalization, and Death by Race/Ethnicity." Centers for Disease Control and Prevention. Last modified March 10, 2022, https:// www.cdc.gov/coronavirus/2019-ncov/covid-data/ investigations-discovery/hospitalization-death-by-race-ethnicity.html.

Collins, William J., and Robert A. Margo. "Race and Home Ownership from the End of the Civil War to the Present," *The American Economic Review* 101, no. 3 (2011): 355.

Early, Dirk W., Paul E. Carrillo, and Edgar O. Olsen. "Racial Rent Differences in U.S. Housing Markets." University of Virginia. June 18, 2018, https://batten. virginia.edu/sites/default/files/2019-09/ECO-DISCRIMINATION-TEXT-TABLES-6-18-18.pdf.

Famighetti, Christopher and Darrick Hamilton. "The Great Recession, education, race, and homeownership." Economic Policy Institute. Last modified 5/15/2019, https://www.epi.org/ blog/the-great-recession-education-race-and-homeownership/.

Goldstein, Ira, and Dan Urevick-Ackelsberg. "Subprime Lending, Mortgage Foreclosures and Race: How far have we come and how far have we to go?" *Where Credit is Due: Bringing Equity to Credit and Housing After the Market Meltdown*, edited by Christy Rogers and John A. Powell, 117–139. Maryland: University Press of America, 2013.

Greene, Solomon and Alanna McCargo. "New Data Suggest COVID-19 is Widening Housing Disparities by Race and Income." Urban Institute. Last modified June 2, 2020, https://www.urban.org/urban-wire/ new-data-suggest-covid-19-widening- housing-disparities-race-and-income.

Hamilton, Darrick, William Darity, Jr., Anne E. Price Vishnu Sridharan, and Rebecca Tippett. "Umbrellas Don't Make it Rain: Why Studying and Working Hard Isn't Enough for Black Americans." The New School. April 2015, http://insightcced.org/wp-content/uploads/ 2015/08/Umbrellas_Dont_Make_It_Rain_Final.pdf.

Immergluck, Dan. "Stark Differences: Explosion of the Subprime Industry and Racial Hypersegmentation in Home Equity Lending." U.S. Department of Housing and Urban Development. https://www.huduser.gov/publications/pdf/brd/11Immer.pdf.

Johnson, Roberta Ann. "African Americans and Homelessness: Moving Through History," *Journal of Black Studies* 40, no. 4 (2010): 583.

Joint Economic Committee, U.S. Congress. "The Economic State of Black America in 2020." Accessed May 1, 2021. https://www.jec.senate.gov/public/_cache/files/ccf4dbe2-810a-44f8-b3e7-14f7e5143ba6/economic-state-of-black-america-2020.pdf.

Liu, Sifan and Joseph Parilla. "New data shows small businesses in communities of color had unequal access to federal COVID-19 relief." Brookings. Last modified September 17, 2020, https://www.brookings.edu/research/new-data-shows-small-businesses-in-communities-of-color-had-unequal-access-to-federal-covid-19-relief/?amp.

Marshall, William F., III "Coronavirus infection by race: What's behind the health disparities?" Mayo Clinic. https://www.mayoclinic.org/diseases-conditions/coronavirus/expert-answers/coronavirus-infection-by-race/faq-20488802.

Traub, Amy, Laura, Sullivan, Tatjana Meschede, and Tom Shapiro. "The Asset Value of Whiteness: Understanding the Racial Wealth Gap." Demos. https://www.demos.org/research/asset-value-whiteness-understanding-racial-wealth-gap.

U.S. Department of Housing and Urban Development. "Unequal Burden: Income and Racial Disparities in Subprime Lending in America," U.S. Department of Housing and Urban Development. Last modified February 22, 2008, https://www.huduser.gov/portal/publications/fairhsg/unequal.html.

Washington, Kemberly. "Covid-19 Has Had A Disproportionate Financial Impact On Black Small Businesses." Forbes. Last modified June 3, 2021, https:// www.forbes.com/advisor/personal-finance/covid19-financial-impact-on-black- businesses/.

World Health Organization. "Global excess deaths associated with COVID-19, January 2020–December 2021: A comprehensive view of global deaths directly and indirectly associated with the COVID-19 Pandemic." World Health Organization. Last modified May, 2022, https://www.who.int/data/stories/global-excess-deaths-associated-with-covid-19-january-2020-december-2021.

ACKNOWLEDGMENTS

When we sat down to write the acknowledgments for this second book, we realized that we had so many people to thank. So many people who believed in this work. So many who opened their homes and shared their stories. So many who wanted to be part of something special and who made this book special with their generosity and sheer authenticity. And honestly, *thank you* feels like two words that are too small to show our appreciation to all who helped make this book a reality.

To the homeowners, you took an incredible journey with us. We reached out to so many of you early on in the pandemic. In a time of uncertainty, you didn't blink when we told you what this book was about and how we wanted to present you in it. From Hawaii to Berlin, you allowed us into your homes and you shared with us the story of your life. Over Zoom you shared with us the intimate stories of where you grew up, but more important, *how* you grew up. You shared the stories of your families, their struggles, and their triumphs. And each story that you told us became its own ethnography, a beautiful study of Black life and Black history. We thank you for being so open. For trusting us with your story. For allowing us to share it here. And we are forever grateful that you allowed us to come into your home during this era of pandemic and opened your hearts to us so we could capture these beautiful and deeply personal images. We know that for each homeowner, this was not easy. But you were each so gracious.

To our editor, Angelin Borsics, you believed in this book from the moment we shared the idea with you. We wanted to write something different: an interiors book, that was equal parts inspirational and historical. We knew that was not an easy task. We thank you for pushing us when we needed pushing. And for giving us the space to write the book we've dreamed of writing. It has been a joy to collaborate with you on our second book together and to create something that is more than a beautiful object, but also a beautiful story that's long needed to be told.

And to the other members of the Potter team: Robert Diaz, we thank you for bringing our images and words to life with such vibrant, creative design for this book and gorgeous typography. Abby Oladipo, we can't thank you enough for your work, overseeing the copyediting and proofreading of this book with such grace and finesse. And to Phil Leung, we thank you for ensuring that this book was printed beautifully.

To our agent, Kim Perel, and the Irene Goodman Literary Agency, we thank you for your excitement and enthusiasm for this book. For recognizing immediately that it was a book that needed to be made. For embracing the vision from the start and helping us to fine-tune it to make this book a reality. For helping us to bring the vision to our publisher and now to this incredible community who will dive deeply into this book, and be inspired by the imagery and stories of these incredible homeowners and the legacy of the Black family home.

To our photographer, Patrick Cline. It's impossible to let you know how truly grateful we are to know you, to have worked with you for over a decade, and to now collaborate again on our second book. One of our dearest friends, there is no one we trusted more to capture the families, their interiors, and to bring their stories to life through photography, than you.

You embraced this project fully, making solo trips around the country to capture each image. We knew we could trust you implicitly and we were not wrong. The images in this book are not only breathtaking, but they show Black life in a way that we haven't seen before in an interiors book—authentic, relaxed, regal, effortless, real. Now that you're gone, we dedicate this book to your memory and the memory of all the times we shared. We're so happy that this book will be a lasting part of your legacy. We will miss you.

To our brand manager, Cheminne Taylor-Smith, this book would not have even been thought of if it were not for you. You listened to the family stories that we would tell. The stories of generations before us and how we were working to preserve homes within our family. You listened and you saw something bigger. You saw that these were stories that needed to be told on a larger scale. And you believed that we were the ones to tell them. Thank you for always seeing and encouraging us. You've helped us grow immensely through the years, helping us embrace our unique voices and perspectives to create a brand that is truly a reflection of the two of us. We thank you for assisting us in identifying families for this book, for taking the time to review and edit along with us. And for always being a sounding board when we needed it and a voice of comfort in challenging times.

And to Charlotte Makhar, Emily Benazzi, and Liz Pezzotta, who helped us find our way to our first home.

There were also some incredibly generous brands that we collaborated with to style some of the interior spaces for this book. They immediately embraced our focus on the Black family home and how their pieces would help tell an important story. We worked with several heritage and artisan brands to bring some of the spaces to life in a way that was sustainable and that supported the purpose of this book. We'd like to thank Bernhardt, Kohler, The Shade Store, Resource Furniture, Perigold, Cambria, Fisher & Paykel, Farrow & Ball, Mitzi, Pottery Barn, Article, and Tuft & Needle for their partnership.

Finally to our families—thank you. We grew up in Pennsylvania in families where home was always there: Mom-Mom's house, Grandmom and Pop-Pop's house, Nana's house, Aunt Laine's house, The House. We know the road was filled with challenges. We know that keeping homes for us to grow up in, play in, make new memories in, was not easy. We know that there was a mountain of discrimination you overcame. And we thank you for your resilience. Because of you, we always knew what home was. In those homes, you instilled so much in us and gave us the vision for this book. Because of you, we hope to help others find home as well.

In Shawna Freeman's home office, leopard print and magenta walls dominate. The painting atop the antique desk, by Kendra Dandy, brings the pattern and color scheme together.